Physical Activity
Ideas for Action

SECONDARY LEVEL

Lynn Allen

Editor

With support from the
Sporting Goods Manufacturers Association (SGMA)

/

Human Kinetics

21182

Library of Congress Cataloging-in-Publication Data

Physical activity ideas for action : secondary level / Lynn Allen,
    editor; with cooperation from the Sporting Goods Manufacturers
    Association (SGMA).
            p.   cm.
        Rev. ed. of: Ideas for action. 1992.
        ISBN 0-88011-555-6
        1. Physical education and training--Study and teaching
(Secondary)--United States.   I. Allen, Lynn, 1958-   .
II. Sporting Goods Manufacturers Association (U.S.)   III. Ideas for
action.
    GV365.P59   1997
    796'.071'2--dc20   96-32474
                                                            CIP
                                                            r96

ISBN: 0-88011-555-6

This book is a revised edition of *Ideas for Action: Award Winning Approaches to Physical Activity*, published in 1992 by the Sporting Goods Manufacturers Association (SGMA).

Acquisitions Editor: Scott Wikgren
Special Projects Editors: Dawn Cassady and Chad Johnson
Editorial Assistants: Amy Carnes and Coree Schutter
Proofreader: Jane Hilken
Graphic Artists: ArtSquare and Francine Hamerski
Text Designer: Judy Henderson
Cover Designer: Jack Davis
Printer: Versa Press

Human Kinetics books are available at special discounts for bulk purchase. Special editions or book excerpts can also be created to specification. For details, contact the Special Sales Manager at Human Kinetics.

Printed in the United States of America   10 9 8 7 6 5 4 3 2 1

Human Kinetics
Web site: http://www.humankinetics.com/

United States: Human Kinetics, P.O. Box 5076, Champaign, IL 61825-5076
1-800-747-4457
e-mail: humank@hkusa.com

Canada: Human Kinetics, Box 24040, Windsor, ON N8Y 4Y9
1-800-465-7301 (in Canada only)
e-mail: humank@hkcanada.com

Europe: Human Kinetics, P.O. Box IW14, Leeds LS16 6TR, United Kingdom
(44) 1132 781708
e-mail: humank@hkeurope.com

Australia: Human Kinetics, 57A Price Avenue, Lower Mitcham, South Australia 5062
(08) 277 1555
e-mail: humank@hkaustralia.com

New Zealand: Human Kinetics, P.O. Box 105-231, Auckland 1
(09) 523 3462
e-mail: humank@hknewz.com

Contents

Preface

The Surgeon General has determined that lack of physical activity is detrimental to your health.

The U.S. Surgeon General feels so strongly about the value of regular physical activity in prolonging and improving life that his office has released the warning printed above: Previous surgeons general had issued warnings only on tobacco and alcohol products. In addition, the Centers for Disease Control and Prevention developed comprehensive physical activity guidelines for youth, recognizing the importance of physical activity. Clearly, the skills, attitudes, and confidence to lead a physically active, healthy life are among the most valuable gifts we can provide our students.

We assembled this book, *Physical Activity Ideas for Action: Secondary Level*, to help you provide these gifts to your students. *Physical Activity Ideas for Action: Secondary Level* is a collection of activities, lesson plans, and spe-

cial events that have been successfully used by physical education teachers across the United States in a wide variety of schools and situations. Even if you have already developed a comprehensive physical activity curriculum, these ideas can enhance your teaching.

We hope you'll find the simple teacher-to-teacher format easy to follow. In essence, this is a cookbook filled with recipes for physical activity that you can use just as they are presented or modify to meet your own tastes.

For easy reference, we've divided the ideas into two parts. Part I provides ideas for middle and junior high school students whereas part II contains ideas for high school students. Many of the ideas can be easily adapted for a higher or lower level. Our goal is to provide a starting point for creating your own new and unique ideas specifically geared to your program.

We hope you will find all the ideas in this book useful to the important work you do. Good luck!

PROMOTION

Tips for Promoting Your Fitness Program

These fitness and activity programs are easily adapted to schools, recreation centers or other organizations interested in promoting fitness. The following information is slanted toward schools, however the principles for promoting fitness programs can be applied to most any type of organization. The real key is planning. As they say, "planning is everything."

Where Do I Start?

The first step is communicating your plans with fellow staff and soliciting their support, as some fellow teachers will become involved in helping promote and conduct the program.

The steps to follow will depend upon the age of the students involved, if you are incorporating a program into the required curriculum, or if it is an optional program students can participate in to increase their activity and fitness levels.

Communicate the program to the students with handouts explaining the program. Have them take the program information home so parents know what you are doing to raise the fitness levels of their children

If the program has opportunity for parent involvement, ask for commitments of time and recommend the way to get the most out of the program as a family.

Publicity

When getting the word out, be sure to present your message attractively. Be innovative but use good taste.

One goal is to create as much visibility as possible, whether promoting only to the students of your school, or promoting to the public.

- Use large, colorful posters located in strategic spots (try churches, libraries, banks, utility companies, public bulletin boards, community buildings, grocery stores...high traffic areas).

- Try handouts at grocery stores, include in student/parent information mailings, etc.

- Take news releases to the local media –newspapers, radio and local and public television stations.(See pages x-xi of this section for a brief overview of how to write a news release or PR release.)

- Build a display in your school.

- Ask to make an announcement in church bulletins, community calendars, and at club meetings.

- Involve key community leaders if the program warrants.

PROMOTING THROUGH THE MEDIA

Developing a relationship with the media

One thing to understand about the media, whether it is newspapers, television or radio, is that the reporter or editor has priorities and deadlines. Know media deadlines and abide by them. A lot of other stories are after the same attention you are, and newspapers only have so much space and radio and television stations only have so much air time they can dedicate to Public Service Announcements (PSAs).

The local newspaper will be your best bet for publicizing your fitness program. They care about what is happening in their local schools, and know their readers care too.

Let's assume you have a press release written and you're ready to take it to the paper. **STOP** right there…did you make an appointment to see the editor? While many people take the route of "dropping off a press release" that's not the way to develop a relationship. Editors, reporters and anchor people are very busy people, but don't think they aren't interested in what you have to say. In fact, they depend on people like you to bring them news. Just remember by setting an appointment you reduce the risk of barging in on someone who is trying to meet a deadline.

You may have to wait, and they may seem abrupt due to a pressing deadline you are unaware of, but be patient…and be helpful by bringing complete information…they'll ask for more but try to make their job easy and you'll have a better chance of gaining their support. Make your presentation as specific as possible. Be sure to include facts as to why your program is interesting and be prepared to offer possible angles the story can be written from. Relate your event to current issues if possible.

If you are mailing the PR release, it will be worth your time to telephone each paper or station you're interested in and get the name of the editor, or news or program director who would be most interested. To make your job easier, keep a list of media contacts typed and labels printed in advance for easy and quick mailing. Time may pass before your information is published or aired, if at all. If considerable time has lapsed, follow-up on your story and supply new or revised data concerning your program, thus keeping it "fresh."

Sometimes it may be necessary to contact the media by phone, such as when following up on the story. When contacting a morning paper by phone, your best bet is mid-to-late afternoon. Afternoon papers usually have deadlines around 11 a.m. so it's best to try after 11:30 a.m. or in the afternoon.

As a general rule in developing important media relations, keep your contacts with media people active on a continuing basis. That doesn't mean becoming a pen pal or a nuisance on the phone. That will have an adverse effect on gaining their support. But a regular flow of news items and personal contact will enhance your chances of getting coverage for your program or event.

If your fitness program calls for involving community leaders, consider the people in the media. They get hundreds of requests, but yours may be one they will respond to.

Quick Tips for Using Press Releases

- Get your release to the media in plenty of time before the event.

- Be professional...never try to get publicity by pressure or through business relationships or friendships.

- Don't ask when a story will appear.

- If you think your story would make a good feature story, rather than a straight news story, ask the editor about it...if it is worthy of space the editor might assign the story and photographs.

- Attribute quotes to the highest ranking person in your organization.

- KITS can be put together when you have a release, photos, a fitness program logo or program materials.

- PHOTOGRAPHS can be effective and are desired. Be sure the photos are clear and show people doing something which is relevant to your story.
  - 8 x 10 or 5 x 7 black and white glossy photos are preferred by newspapers
  - when possible work with the newspaper photographer and set up each shot
  - try to limit the number of people in each shot to three unless you want a crowd shot
  - involve subjects in an activity–choose an interesting background but avoid clutter–provide props
  - identify all people and places in your photos–type the information on a gummed label or piece of paper and affix it to the back of photo and submit it with your press release

Other Ideas for Publicizing Your Fitness Program or Event

- Radio or television talk shows.

- Consider cable television which offers 24-hour community news channels to publicize events and projects (contact the person in charge of local programming).

- Build displays or exhibits in shopping malls, banks, store windows, churches, recreation centers, utility companies, at school open house, PTA meetings, etc.– look professional.

- If you need community support, speak at local service club meetings.

- Develop posters–use talents of students, art classes, art teachers, etc. Make posters colorful and creative. Hang them in offices, store windows, bowling alleys, churches, supermarkets, schools, libraries, bookstores, restaurants, etc.

- Create fitness buttons and distribute to students, planners, staff, teachers, etc.

- Send flyers home with students.

```
Your Name
Title
School/Organization
Address
City/State/Zip
Phone                                    FOR IMMEDIATE RELEASE
```

GUIDELINES FOR WRITING PRESS RELEASES

YOUR TOWN, State- Suggestions for preparing and placing a news release or PR release are being outlined here today in the Physical Activity Ideas For Action manual, for teachers to read and use as guidelines when promoting their fitness programs.

Releases should be typed and photocopied cleanly on white 8 1/2" x 11" paper. Mail them first class to the media in your area, including radio and television news directors and local newspapers. It's best to deliver a copy personally to city editors of local newspapers.

Other guidelines:

IDENTIFICATION: The name, organization, address and telephone number of the person to contact for more information should appear at upper left.

RELEASE DATE: Your release should be immediate. If you are submitting the news release prior to an event for publication immediately after the event, use a hold release and be specific: FOR RELEASE AFTER 8:00 P.M. THURSDAY, MARCH 7, 1996.

SPACING: Use wide margins, 1 1/2 inches, so editors can write in them, AND double space so editors can edit the story.

-more-

Release Guidelines
Page 2

HEADLINES: Write an eye-catching headline that is to the point. Some editors will rewrite the headline. Leave about 2 inches between release line and body of copy so editor can insert or rewrite their headline. If you do include a headline, type it in all capital letters and center it.

SUMMARY LEAD: In the first paragraph, try to include the who, what, when, where type of information. Editors expect the most important information to be at the beginning and will often start cutting copy from the bottom up. Use a lead that will catch and hold a busy reader's attention. Use short, punchy sentences.

LENGTH: If it is a news release, keep it to one or two pages–features two to three. Edit your material to bare facts and make sure it is accurate, timely and newsworthy. Do not split a paragraph between the first and second page. When you get to an inch from the bottom of the page and still have more copy, center the word "-more-" to indicate the story continues. At the top left of the second sheet, type a 2 or 3 word description of article and page number.

ACCURACY: Make sure spelling and grammar are 100% accurate. Proofread very carefully. Double check your facts.

PLACEMENT: Take your press release to local newspapers, television and radio stations. Discuss special news with special-ized writers. Never take the same story twice to the same place.

At the end of your release, center the editorial symbol for "the end" which is either -30- or ### at the bottom of the page.

###

PUBLIC SERVICE ANNOUNCEMENTS (PSAs)

Both radio and television utilize Public Service Announcements which are free to non-profit organizations. Here is the basic information about PSAs.

- Contact the radio station 2-5 weeks in advance of when you want it to air.

- Approach area radio and television stations for taping local PSAs and creating artwork–use local personalities, students, or committee chairs in your PSAs.

- Send a thank you letter to the public service director and let him/her know the favorable comments and results you've received with the PSA.

Radio

Copy for radio is written differently than for print media, but it should still contain the same facts: who, what, when, where, why and how.

Consider the format and audience of each radio station (top 40, country, news, etc.) and choose stations most suited to your message.

- Write in a conversational style.

- Spell out all numbers, etc, for reading.

- If you have difficult or unusual names or words, provide the phonetic pronunciations.

- Double or triple space copy.

- Use wide margins for editing.

- In upper left hand corner where you type your name and organization, include start and stop dates for airing as they pertain to your program or event. Also include the number of words in the PSA to help the program director gauge the reading time.

- To make sure your information is easy to read and understand, try reading copy aloud to someone else for their input. Approximate PSA times for radio:
  10 seconds (25 words of copy)
  20 seconds (50 words of copy)
  30 seconds (75 words of copy)
  60 seconds (150 words of copy)

With radio you can also add music or sound effects, include voices from students, etc. If you check with the public service director, they may professionally produce a spot for you at no charge.

Television

This is a visual and audio medium, so write the copy from a conversational style for the announcer, and provide if possible, a slide, good photo or program logo that perhaps a school child drew for them to show on the television screen. Use art that is simple yet conveys your message. Ask for assistance from the station's art department if needed. Tie art work or slides into your program for publicity continuity.

- Meet with the station's public service director to explain your ideas and find out what would be the best for promoting your organization.

- Television hits the highlights so provide the most interesting and visual aspects of your unique fitness program.

- Approximate PSA times for television:
  10 seconds (25 words of copy)
  20 seconds (45 words of copy)
  30 seconds (65 words of copy)
  60 seconds (125 words of copy)

You'll find the number of words for television is less than for radio because television copy is read slower.

PROMOTING TO PARENTS

Here is a sample letter you may use as a guide for informing parents of the program and/or soliciting their involvement. In addition, to sustain interest in the fitness program, consider sending positive notes or making phone calls to parents regarding the student's progress and achievements. The challenge is to improve attitudes toward fitness in both the students and the parents.

Dear Parents:

Your son or daughter will be participating in a new physical fitness program soon. The name of the program is (FILL IN THE NAME OF YOUR PROGRAM) . It will begin on (date) and run approximately _____ weeks.

(DESCRIBE THE PROGRAM ie. In this program, we will explore a wide variety of topics related to health, physical fitness and emphasis will be placed on establishing healthy habits that will last a lifetime. Students will learn how to assess their own level of fitness based on the knowledge gained in this program and be able to design their own personal fitness plan. They will learn to maintain the desired level of physical fitness once it is reached. Some topics we will discuss include etc. etc. We will have a guest speaker…etc.)

Your child will be involved in a wide range of fitness activities. The weekly schedule is set up for # days of activity and # days of classroom sessions. Students will be expected to perform only at their own level. Our goal is to help each student strive for and recognize gains in his or her fitness level.

If you have questions or would like to have further information about this program, please contact me by phone or letter. Soon you will be receiving information about (Family Fitness Night (use the name of your family involvement night if you have one) which will be held (date if known or semester). Your attendance will be greatly appreciated. We hope you can join us and show your support and give encouragement to your child for continued good work toward improving their health and fitness.

As always, I welcome you to stop by any time and see what is happening at the (YOUR SCHOOL) Physical Education Department.

Sincerely,

PLANNING

Planning Calendar for "A Year of Fitness"

Source: NASPE Fit To Achieve Program
Here are some ideas from NASPE to consider when planning your Year of Fitness:

January
- Begin planning special events and activities relating to National Physical Fitness & Sports Month and National Physical Education & Sports Week: May 1 thru 7.
- Present a physical education class demonstration at the local high school basketball game during the halftime program to educate the public about today's physical education curriculum.
- Plan a Jump Rope Demo for your school and publicize the benefits of jumping rope in PTA Newsletter and local newspaper.

February
- Celebrate National Girls and Women in Sports Day, Feb. 6. National Association for Girls & Women in Sport, 1900 Association Drive, Reston, VA 22091. (703) 476-3452. Materials: Community Action Kit.
- Hold a "Jump Rope for Heart" event to raise money for cardiovascular research.

March
- Attend the state/district and/or national meetings of the American Alliance for Health, Physical Education, Recreation and Dance.
- Participate in or plan a local health/fitness fair by disseminating information about the need for quality, daily physical education and providing demonstrations.

April
- Inform parents about the upcoming youth fitness assessments through a ditto or school's PTA News. Explain the purpose of the assessments, recommended outcomes and how the results impact your teaching plans.
- Invite parents to help you as aides during the testing to record results, set up materials, etc.

May
- As a part of National Physical Fitness & Sports Month, encourage classroom teachers to have students do a classroom exercise about the importance of good physical fitness, i.e., an essay on personal thoughts, a story about physical challenges, a report on a sport, a picture or a math or science exercise.
- For information about National Running and Fitness Week, May 10–17, contact: American Running and Fitness Association, 4405 East West Highway, Suite 405, Bethesda, MD 20814; (301) 913-9517. Materials: press releases, posters.
- Promote a parent/student physical fitness activity for the whole school to do, i.e. a school walk.

June
- Coordinate a school field day activity and invite parents to come and help.
- Offer special fitness and physical activity suggestions for the whole family to do over the summer months in a special ditto or school's PTA news.

July
- Join the National Association for Sport and Physical Education (NASPE) and the American Alliance for Health, Physical Education, Recreation and Dance (AAHPERD) to learn about the latest developments in your profession and to network with colleagues around the country.

September
- Plan to make opportunities throughout the school year to speak to groups of parents, i.e., at PTA meetings or back-to-school nights. NASPE has available for sale a 20-minute slide presentation about the importance of quality physical education programs. A 12-minute video, "The Case for Daily Physical Education," is also available.
- Inform parents about the upcoming fitness assessments through a ditto or school's PTA News. Explain the purpose of the tests, recommended outcomes and how the results impact your teaching plans.
- Distribute a checklist for parents so they can help increase the physical activity their children get, and assist in making good diet choices, etc.

October
- Present a physical education class exercise at the local high school football game during the halftime program to educate the public about today's physical education curriculum.

November
- Tell a colleague about the resources available by joining the National Association for Sport and Physical Education (NASPE).

December
- Invite local college/university physical education professors to observe as well as participate in your physical education class.

EXAMPLE

MAY
National Physical Fitness and Sports Month

SUNDAY	MONDAY	TUESDAY	WEDNESDAY	THURSDAY	FRIDAY	SATURDAY
			1 Jump rope for 3 minutes	**2** Perform 5 sit-ups	**3** Run around your house 5 times	**4** Kick an empty milk jug using soccer dribbling skills around your house 3 times
5 Ride your bike or skateboard with a friend	**6** Perform 5 push-ups	**7** Perform 20 jumping jacks	**8** Perform 20 toe touches from sitting position	**9** Skip around your house 5 times with dog	**10** Walk around in your yard with a friend for 15 minutes or longer	**11** Shoot basketball by yourself or with a friend or toss a ball to yourself and catch it
12 Give your mother 5 hugs throughout the day and tell her "Happy Mother's Day"	**13** Throw and catch a ball with a friend for 15 minutes or longer	**14** Practice sit and reach by touching your toes. Remember to keep your legs straight! Do 5 times	**15** Perform 10 sit-ups	**16** Run around your house 10 times	**17** Perform 10 push-ups	**18** Hit a baseball back & forth over a net, chair or some other object with a friend, like playing volleyball! 15 min. or longer
19 Perform 20 toe touches from sitting position	**20** Bounce a ball while running in a zig zag pattern for 10 minutes or longer	**21** Perform 35 jumping jacks	**22** Practice your forward roll, perform 5 of them. Practice your balance skills by walking on a straight line	**23** Jump rope for 5 minutes	**24** Jump up and down 20 times because it's Friday	**25** Kick a ball back and forth with a friend for 15 minutes or longer
26 Kick a ball to a target–hit target 10 times	**27** Perform 15 sit-ups	**28** Kick an empty milk jug using soccer dribbling skills around your house 5 times	**29** Perform 50 Jumping jacks	**30** Perform 10 arm circles in forward direction with palms up–then 10 arm circles in backward direction, palms down	**31** Give yourself a pat on the back for all your hard work this month	

SAMPLE

	SATURDAY				
	FRIDAY				
	THURSDAY				
	WEDNESDAY				
	TUESDAY				
	MONDAY				
	SUNDAY				

Part I

Middle School Program Ideas

A Cooperative Approach to Fitness Practice

School: Seven Oaks Elementary School
9220 Seven Courts Drive
Baltimore, MD 21236
Phone: (410) 887-6257
Contributor: Susan P. Kogut–NASPE NATIONAL TEACHER OF THE YEAR

Program Objectives

- to enhance fitness of middle and secondary students through a team approach

- to motivate students to practice fitness while encouraging others

- to make fitness fun

- to improve rapport among students

Materials/Equipment Needed

- track or marked course

- gymnasium (or recreation area)

- deck of playing cards

- sports equipment (balls, climbing rope)

- balloons

- music and tape player

- index cards for record keeping

Procedures and Teaching Strategies

- use cooperative activities to build on the team concept and make fitness fun

Program Description

Cooperative learning and cooperative activities work best with a group of four (4) students. The **"quad"** can replace the traditional **"squad."** The groups can learn to work as a team as they solve problems, practice skills and enhance fitness.
The ideas presented are for groups of four (4) students to practice and improve fitness together.

CARDIOVASCULAR FITNESS

A. Run Rummy – Each lap of a track or measured course that is completed by each team member is rewarded with a playing card. The team must compare and combine cards as they run to accumulate a "run" (a series of consecutive cards). The length of the run, required suits, etc. can be determined by the teacher based on the level of the group.

B. Aerobic Quad Share – Each quad selects a favorite song and creates an aerobic routine to it. Each quad leads their own original routine. The entire class does all of the routines, thus creating an entire workout. Less vigorous ones can be selected or planned for the warm up and cool down segments of this complete workout session.

MUSCULAR ENDURANCE

A. Circle Sit-ups – All four (4) students are in the sit-up position with their toes in to the center of the circle. As the sit-ups are performed, a ball is passed or a ball or balloon is volleyed to each player. Consecutive catches/hits can be counted. Several balls or balloons can be added based on the skill and level of the group. Music adds to the fun and excitement of this activity.

B. Group Juggling – Start in the same team position as above. Start with one (1) ball and pass to player 2, then to player 3, then to player 4, and finally back to player 1. A pattern is established and repeated. As the team is successful, a second, third and fourth ball can be added.

MUSCULAR STRENGTH

A. Cumulative Chin-ups or Push-ups Have an index card for each quad and have a daily time (preferably during warm-up) where teams establish team goals and accumulate a team total for the day. Keep a running record of team's total improvement toward goal.

B. Other Activities – Team totals canbe recorded for other strength activities such as hanging time, rope climbing or other gymnastic skills.

Program Results

This team approach created new enthusiasm for fitness practice and improvement. Students improved their self-esteem while encouraging others to improve and work toward shared goals and objectives.

Program Tips

Set individual and team goals so the team members support each other as they progress.

Record class total at the end of each quarter to gauge improvement.

Fitness Activities to Start Your Day

School: University of North Carolina, Wilmington
601 South College Road
Wilmington, NC 28403-3297
Phone: (910) 395-3740
Contributor: John P. Bennett, Ed.D. Associate Professor, HPER Dept.

Program Objectives

- to engage all students in activities that promote overall fitness development

- to involve students in activities that not only allow for entry level by skill level, but that will help to assist students in learning fitness principles in a fun-filled, non-threatening environment

- to provide an opportunity for all students to be viewed as being successful and engaged in positive social situations in the physical education classroom

Materials/Equipment Needed

- tape player

- taped music with intervals

- gymnasium (or recreation area)

- station cards

- various station equipment – cones, jump ropes, hand weights, mats

Procedures and Teaching Strategies

- utilize both student and teacher in program design

- delivery system is a practice style which allows and promotes maximum success and on task time for all students

- activities are designed as "opening activities" to engage students quickly into the learning environment

Program Description

This is a package of five (5) fitness activities with which most physical educators are quite familiar. However, in this package the activities have been developed with both sport skills and rhythmic/dance/gymnastic skills in mind. All of the physical organizational patterns will appear very familiar, however, the intent of this material is to open the user up to new ways to utilize some of the traditional organizational patterns of the past in new and exciting ways with the students. These patterns are most often labeled as circuits/stations.

The circuit can be conducted in a variety of ways. Students can move on a signal from the instructor. Taped music with intervals works well as a signaling device while providing a motivational factor. The instructor could also assign a given number of repetitions to be completed at each station before advancement. Another option might be to have all participants go to the center of the gymnasium for a session of aerobics between stations. Students could also run/walk laps around the gymnasium between stations. (30 - 60 seconds per station, depending on the ability of the class, is a good time limit for the intervals.)

Program Results

The results were exactly the ones that everyone wants in specific parts of their lessons. The on task time was very high, learning new skills in fun and exciting ways was present, and students were able to interact in new and exciting relationships. A final dividend is that you, as the teacher, were able to set up situations in your classes that helped promote the making of connections to the entire spectrum of skills; it's called "natural integration."

Program Tips

Share directions for the activities with student's home base teacher.

Post directions in locker rooms, outside your classroom and/or on the wall in your classroom.

Have students **work in groups** to develop their own set of learning experiences.

Develop a writing activity in which students share their thoughts on this activity.

Modify activities as necessary to include all ages.

Four Wall 1

FOUR WALL

- Go into room and start walking or jogging.

- On the signal to begin, move to the center of the room and face wall A.

- Begin at level A1 with the music and on signal turn to wall B and do level B1.

- Continue turning right on the signal and moving down the list C1, D1, A2, B2, etc.

Four Wall 2

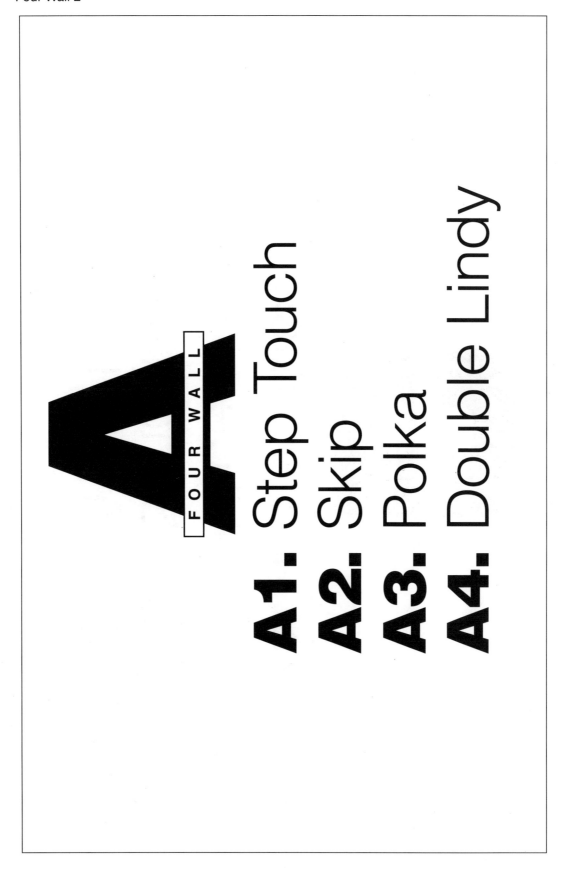

FOUR WALL

A1. Step Touch

A2. Skip

A3. Polka

A4. Double Lindy

Four Wall 2

Four Wall 3

Four Wall 4

FOUR WALL

C1. Side Touch

C2. Gallop

C3. Two-Step

C4. Shag

Four Wall 5

FOUR WALL

D1. Heel Shuffle

D2. Run

D3. Cha Cha Cha

D4. Grapevine

Four Corners 1

FOUR CORNERS

- Go into room and start walking or jogging.

- Go to a corner on the signal and start around the room clockwise following directions.

- Move around the room clockwise at your own pace.

- No more than 10 or 12 people start in each corner.

Four Corners 2

CORNER 1

1st time: Skip

2nd time: Run and turn

3rd time: Schottische

↑

Four Corners 3

CORNER 2

1st time: Gallop

2nd time: Grapevine

3rd time: Two-step

Four Corners 4

CORNER 3

1st time: Slide

2nd time: Schottische with turns

3rd time: Double Texas two-step

Four Corners 5

CORNER 4

1st time: Run and leap

2nd time: Skip and turn

3rd time: Polka

Stations (A-H) 1

STATIONS (A-H)

- Go into room and start walking or jogging.

- Go to a station on the signal and begin the activity.

- No more than 5 people per station.

- Switch stations on the signal (option: run one or two laps around the room and stop at the next station or go to the center for aerobics).

- Move around the room clockwise.

Stations (A-H) 2

A. SHUTTLE STATION

- Move between the markers touching an imaginary line between them.

- Move forward, backward, sideways, turning, changing patterns (skip, gallop, schottische, etc.).

- Repeat the sequence over and over until the next signal, then move to the next station.

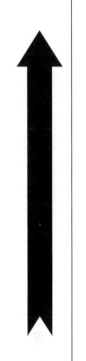

Stations (A-H) 3

B. FLEXIBILITY

Hip Girdle Stretching

- Select your own.
- Slow, gentle static stretching.
- Move on signal to next station.

Stations (A-H) 4

C. CRABWALK

- Crabwalk between markers.

- First go forward, then backward, and then sideways.

- Repeat over and over until next signal and then move on to next station.

Stations (A-H) 5

D. JUMP AND REACH

- Practice vertical jump over and over.
- Practice standing long jump over and over for distance.
- Move on signal to next station.

E. SIT-UPS

- Slow continuous movement.
- Do as many as you can until the next signal to move on.

Stations (A-H) 7

F. FLEXIBILITY

Shoulder Girdle Stretching

- Select your own.
- Slow, gentle static stretching.
- Move on signal to the next station.

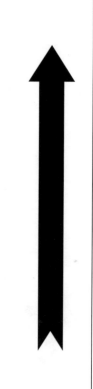

Stations (A-H) 8

G. WALK ON ALL FOURS

- Walk on all fours back and forth between the markers.

- First go forward, then backward, and then sideways.

- Repeat over and over until the next signal and then move on to the next station.

Stations (A-H) 9

H. ROPE JUMPING

- Continuous turning of the rope until the next signal (utilize a variety of turns and jumps).

CIRCUIT (1-8) 1

CIRCUIT (1-8)

- Go into room and start walking or jogging.
- Go to station when music changes and start.
- No more than 5 people per station.
- 1-10 repetitions of each exercise and no more than double.
- Switch stations when you are ready (option: run one or two laps around the room and stop at next station or go to center of room for aerobics).
- Move around the room clockwise.

CIRCUIT (1-8) 2

1. ABDOMINALS

- Curl-ups.
- Crunches.
- Knee-to-chest twists.

CIRCUIT (1-8) 3

2. ARMS

- Push-ups.
- Crab push-ups.
- Pull-ups.

CIRCUIT (1-8) 4

3. QUADRICEPS

- Plies.
- Plie position and bounce ball off wall 1-20 times.

CIRCUIT (1-8) 5

4. JUMP ROPE

- Continuous movement forward and backward with varying patterns.

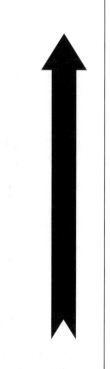

CIRCUIT (1-8) 6

5. UPPER BACK RHOMBOIDS

- Bent knees and leaning slightly forward, "flys" with weights, 1–20 times.

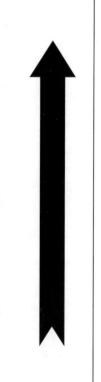

CIRCUIT (1-8) 7

6. CHEST

- Lie on bench or floor and do "flys" with weights, 1-20 times.

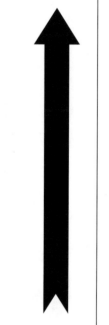

CIRCUIT (1-8) 8

7. AEROBIC

- Gallop, slide, and skip through the open spaces.

CIRCUIT (1-8) 9

8. LINE TOUCH

- Run back and forth between the lines touching the line with your hand each time 1-20 times.

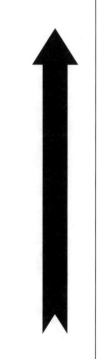

COUNTDOWN 1

COUNTDOWN

- Go into room and start walking or jogging around the outside of the room/markers.

- On the signal, start following directions and work your way from the 'jog 5 laps' sign down to the 'jog 1 lap' sign.

- Don't do more than twice the suggested number of repetitions.

- Work at your own pace.

COUNTDOWN 2

JOG 1 LAP
OR
AEROBICS 1 MINUTE

- Rope jump forward 1-30X.
- Rope jump backward 1-30X.

COUNTDOWN 3

JOG 2 LAPS OR AEROBICS 2 MINUTES

- Balance standing still, each leg 15 seconds.
- Mule kicks, 1-15X.

COUNTDOWN 4

JOG 3 LAPS
OR
AEROBICS 3 MINUTES

- Long sit, single leg lifts 1-10X each leg.

- Fire hydrants, 1-10X each leg.

COUNTDOWN 5

JOG 4 LAPS
OR
AEROBICS 4 MINUTES

- Push-ups, 1-10X.
- Crab push-ups, 1-10X.

COUNTDOWN 6

JOG 5 LAPS
OR
AEROBICS 5 MINUTES

- Crunches, 1–10X.
- Knee to chest twists, 1–10X each side.

Fitness Course Markers

School: Pennsylvania College of Technology–Penn State
1004 Locust Street
Williamsport, PA
Phone: (717) 322-3910
Contributor: Paul "Babe" Mayer–NASPE TEACHER OF THE YEAR

Program Objectives

• to create innovative exercise courses regardless of facility limitations

• to promote individual student learning strategies

• to diminish the monotony of repeating activities on a set track

Materials/Equipment Needed

• measuring wheel

• FITNESS COURSE MARKERS

• fitness monitoring charts

• stop watches

• erasable markers

Procedures and Teaching Strategies

• using FITNESS MARKERS allows the instructor to create lessons that focus on individual learning processes while freeing the instructor to assist where needed most

• provide students with explicit instructions for completing tasks at a level suited to personal abilities and needs

• instructor can create innovative courses and lessons to challenge students without being the central figure in class regulation

Program Description

The use of FITNESS COURSE MARKERS allows the instructor the flexibility of creating different and innovative exercise courses. This eliminates the boredom of exercising on the same course, while challenging the students to navigate new courses. The MARKERS display a numbered sequence, distance covered, and direction to the next marker. The distance can be quickly measured by using a measuring wheel. Simple to difficult courses incorporating various terrains can be created. The markers are placed in sequence along a designated course where students visually observe the marker to navigate the course.

FITNESS MARKERS are best used when teaching long distance aerobic activities, i.e.: fitness walking, jogging, cycling, roller skating, swimming, hiking and cross-country skiing. FITNESS MARKERS can be used with other aerobic activities by adapting the content headings to apply to appropriate measurements.

Suggested Progression of Activities

The FITNESS MARKERS can be introduced to the students in the following progression: fitness course navigation, pacing, measuring target heart rates, and calculating caloric expenditure. The instructor should explain the lesson, lead the class through the lesson, then allow the students to experiment with the lesson content. Once the four components are covered, the instructor then assigns the students the task of developing a program that suits individual abilities and needs.

FITNESS COURSE MARKER # _____

DISTANCE
_____ Mile(s)
_____ Feet
_____ Meters

PACE TIME
__·__ MPH __:__
__·__ MPH __:__
__·__ MPH __:__

PERFORM
_____ Warm Up
_____ Pulse Count
_____ Kcal Expenditure
_____ Cool Down

DIRECTION

Pacing

Pacing is an essential component of exercising. Understanding pace aids in overcoming the urge to exert a maximum effort at the beginning of a workout that could otherwise result in negative outcomes. Pacing skills balance the workout to achieve the maximum training effect. FITNESS COURSE MARKERS placed at equal intervals throughout a course allow the students to visually compare actual time expired to desired pace time. The FITNESS COURSE MARKERS allow the instructor to display 3 MPH/pace times appropriate to the activity. The student then makes adjustments to achieve a desired pace. Pace is specific to the activity, but simple calculations can produce charts like the one below.

	1/10 MILE	1/4 MILE	1 MILE
SAMPLE WALKING PACE CHART			
Speed	**Pace Time**	**Pace Time**	**Pace Time**
3.5 MPH	1:43	4:17	17:08
4.0 MPH	1:30	3:45	15:00
4.5 MPH	1:00	3:20	13:20

Measuring Target Heart Rate

An aerobic exercise is one that creates a cardiovascular training effect. This means the exercise intensity is 60%-80% of maximum, the duration is a minimum of 20 minutes and the frequency is 3 to 5 days per week. Duration and frequency are easy to understand and evaluate, but intensity is a different matter. What is 60%-80% of maximum? This means an exercise heart rate should fall within this range. A simple formula can establish an individual's target heart rate range (SEE CHART 1. CALCULATING TARGET HEART RATE RANGE). Once the range is determined, the student can measure their exercise heart rate throughout the exercise session (SEE CHART 2. EVALUATING EXERCISE HEART RATES) and determine if the exercise intensity is sufficient. Checking the "pulse count" box on the FITNESS COURSE MARKER directs the student to measure exercise heart rate, six second pulse, at intervals designated by the instructor. The student can then evaluate and adjust workouts appropriately.

Calculating Caloric Expenditure

Body composition intervention strategies are directly related to aerobic exercising. Aerobic exercise burns calories, aids in behavior modification, and enhances self image which are all important components of weight control. A sound body composition intervention strategy combines a 50% focus on reducing caloric intake and a 50% focus on increasing caloric expenditure, with a one pound weekly fat loss goal. This strategy helps the body to adjust to the change. Since one pound of fat is equal to 3500 calories, the daily caloric deficit would then equal 500 calories, 250 calories from the diet and 250 from exercising. Decreasing 250 calories from the diet can be approached in several ways, the simplest being to reduce the portions of foods you normally eat. Exercising away 250 calories can be measured by referring to a caloric expenditure chart (SEE CHART 3). Excellent individual problem solving tasks can be devised to determine calories expended during exercise and developing personalized intervention strategies. Remember, expending 250 calories can be divided into several daily exercise sessions. Checking the "caloric output" box on the FITNESS COURSE MARKER directs the students to measure caloric expenditure. The students can then evaluate and adjust workouts appropriately (SEE CHART 4).

SAMPLE

Chart 1

Calculating Target Heart Rate Range

NAME _____ DATE_____ CLASS_____

Purpose: To identify a target heart rate zone which is a safe and comfortable level of overload that should be maintained to achieve a training effect.

Procedure: Study the example provided before completing this activity.

	EXAMPLE	FOR YOU LOWER LIMIT	UPPER LIMIT
START WITH 220	220	220	220
SUBTRACT YOUR AGE	-12	-_____	-_____
EQUALS MAXIMUM HEART RATE (MHR)	208	=_____	=_____
MAXIMUM TIMES HEART SHOULD BEAT/MIN. SUBTRACT RESTING HEART RATE	-72	-_____	-_____
MULTIPLY BY: 60% – LOWER LIMIT 80% – UPPER LIMIT	136 X .60	_____ X .60	_____ X .80
ADD RESTING HEART RATE	81.60 +72	=_____ +_____	=_____ +_____
EQUALS TARGET HEART RATE (THR)	153 BEATS PER MINUTE		

YOUR THR

Chart 2

EVALUATING EXERCISE HEART RATES

	Workout 1	Workout 2	Workout 3	Workout 4
Record EHR	1. _____	1. _____	1. _____	1. _____
(6 sec. pulse	2. _____	2. _____	2. _____	2. _____
times 10)	3. _____	3. _____	3. _____	3. _____
Workout Average =	_____	_____	_____	_____

Chart 3

CALORIES EXPENDED PER MINUTE FOR VARIOUS BODY WEIGHTS AND TARGET HEART RATES

BODY WEIGHT

THR	90	100	110	120	130	140	150	160	170	180	190	200	210	220
60%	8	9	10	10	11	11	12	13	13	14	14	15	16	16
70%	10	10	11	12	12	13	14	14	15	16	16	17	18	19
80%	11	12	12	14	14	15	16	16	17	18	19	19	20	21

KCAL EXPENDED PER MINUTE

Chart 4

EVALUATING CALORIC EXPENDITURE

Kcal Expended/Minute X Duration = Caloric Expenditure

SAMPLE

FITNESS COURSE MARKER # _____

DISTANCE
____ Mile(s)
____ Feet
____ Meters

PACE TIME
____ . ____ MPH ____ : ____
____ . ____ MPH ____ : ____
____ . ____ MPH ____ : ____

PERFORM
____ Warm Up
____ Pulse Count
____ Kcal Expenditure
____ Cool Down

DIRECTION

I'm No Middle School Couch Potato

School: Bettendorf Middle School
2030 Middle Rd.
Bettendorf, IA 52722
Phone: (319) 359-3686
Contributor: Regina McGill–NASPE TEACHER OF THE YEAR

Program Objectives

• to instill in students the value of healthy life style choices, especially regular exercise

• to help students to understand the relationship between worthy use of leisure time and overall good health, physical and mental well-being

• to upgrade fitness level of students

• to improve rapport among students, parents and teachers

Materials/Equipment Needed

• aerobic instructor and an organizer/ leader(s) of the program

• gymnasium (or recreation area)

• designated hallways for walking/ jogging or other physical activity

• sports equipment (balls, nets, etc.)

• provide for activities like jogging, walking, calisthenics, aerobic dance, use of weight machines and free weights, basketball and volleyball

Procedures and Teaching Strategies

• use goals and rewards to promote physical fitness in and outside the gymnasium

• involve Middle School students and parents

• urge co-workers to become involved

• schedule speakers and videos for informational sessions on fitness-related activities

Program Description

This is an enrichment program where students/teachers and parents can utilize school facilities one night a week. Students are encouraged to participate regardless of parental involvement. For the first 20-25 minutes, participants do aerobic activity such as walking or running. Then they are split into groups to do a variety of activities such as basketball, volleyball, aerobic dance, swimming, weight training, calisthenics, etc. Each program night the student/teacher attends, he/she earns ten (10) points. If parent(s) attend, the student earns two (2) bonus points. Participants sign the register each activity night to claim their points.

Participants can earn additional points each week by selecting from the activities listed. The selected activity must be performed continuously for the time indicated. Five (5) points are earned when the participant performs the activity outside of school hours with an additional two (2) bonus points if a parent participates with the student.

An exercise diary and fitness point chart are kept by the participants. Maximum points participants can earn in one week total 26.

- attendance one night/week at school with parent = 12 points

- two activity sessions during the week from the list performed with parent = 14 points

When participants earn 100 points, they receive a "I'm No Middle School Couch Potato" T-shirt. T-shirts are awarded during the last five minutes of activity night.

Activities	Number of Minutes
Walking	30
Jogging	20
Rope Jumping	10
Bicycle Riding	30
Swimming	15
Soccer	20
Basketball	30
Aerobics	20
Cross Country Skiing	20
Other	Ask Instructor

Program Results

Target goal was to involve 200-250 students with parents and one-third of school staff. Actual participation was 180-200 Middle School students; 30-40 brothers and sisters; 60-70 parents; 15 staff/teachers.

Over two-thirds of students involved were 6th graders.

T-shirts earned: 168 Middle School students; 15 faculty

Many students participating were not involved in interscholastics or intramurals–so another segment of the student population was reached.

Program Tips

Guest speakers might include well-known athletes from a local college (ie. a cross-country champion, baseball player, etc. whose sport is "off season" at the time of your program); a local physician, nurse or health care professional; past professional sports players who may live in the community, etc.

Awards such as T-shirts and printed certificates may be funded by a grant avail-able through your state associations, ie. the District Association for Health, Physical Education, Recreation and Dance; or donation by a local company. Consider allowing brothers/sisters/parents to buy T–shirts with money going back into the account that funds the awards.

Promote the program as much as possible through local newspapers and TV. Send press releases to these media with a copy of the program graphic to launch the program. Make a friendly contact at the paper and arrange for them to do follow-up stories occasionally to report how the program is working out.

Program graphic can be used as the T–shirt design and used with newspaper stories, TV story, informational materials to send home with the child, school banners/posters, etc. It may be donated by the art teacher, local college art class or design studio, or opened up as a middle school art contest (five dollars as prize and possibly name in paper).

Plan for evenings when the program may get pushed out of the gymnasium due to other planned events such as freshman games and meets.

S A M P L E
S I D E   1

"I'm No Middle School Couch Potato"

(Date)

Dear Students and Teachers:

"I'm No Middle School Couch Potato" is a fitness/wellness program for Middle School students, staff and parents. This program will be held on Monday nights at the Middle School gymnasium from 7:15 – 8:15 p.m. starting (date   ) and continuing through (date   ). The purpose of the program is to help students learn about life style choices and to get students, their parents and staff involved in regular exercise activities. Students are encouraged to invite parents to participate in the program, but it is not a requirement.

The educational components of the program will include guest speakers and videos while activities will include jogging, walking, calisthenics, aerobic dance, use of weight machines, free weights, basketball and volleyball. Each night will consist of 20-25 minutes of aerobic activity followed by various sports activities. Students and teachers involved in the program can earn an "I'm No Middle School Couch Potato" T-Shirt. Bonus points will be earned by students when their parents participate with them.

We are excited about the program and hope you will actively participate. Join in so you can earn points to wear an "I'm No Middle School Couch Potato" T-shirt and be fit!!

Enjoy a QUALITY LIFESTYLE – And BE A WINNER!

Yours in fitness,

(Signature)

DIRECTIONS: The "I'm No Middle School Couch Potato" program is designed to improve your aerobic fitness and make your heart and lungs stronger. Each Monday night you participate in the activities at the Middle School gymnasium you will earn 10 points. If parents attend and participate you will get 2 extra bonus points. You may earn additional points each week by selecting from the activities listed below. The selected activity should be performed continuously for the time indicated. You earn 5 points when you perform the activity after school hours, and 2 bonus points if a parent participates with you. You may earn no more than 14 points per week from the list of activities. Keep track of your points on your exercise diary and fitness point chart.

The MAXIMUM number of points you can earn any one week is 26. Attending activities at Middle School on Monday night with a parent earns 12 points, and choosing an activity and doing it continuously for the time indicated with a parent two different nights after school hours earns 7 points each night. Each time you do activities outside of school have your parents sign your exercise diary. Each Monday night you attend activities at the gym you will sign in to claim your points.

When you earn 100 points you will receive a "I'm No Middle School Couch Potato" T-shirt.

Activities	Number of Minutes
Walking	30
Jogging	20
Rope Jumping	10
Bicycle Riding	30
Swimming	15
Soccer	20
Basketball	30
Aerobics	20
Cross Country Skiing	20
Other*	

* If you have questions on other activities, please contact _____

SAMPLE

Quality Lifestyle
"I'm No Middle School Couch Potato"
Exercise Diary

Name _____ Grade _____

Activity	How Long	With Whom	Points Earned	Verification

SAMPLE

1	2	3	4	5	6	7	8	9	10
11	12	13	14	15	16	17	18	19	20
21	22	23	24	25	26	27	28	29	30
31	32	33	34	35	36	37	38	39	40
41	42	43	44	45	46	47	48	49	50
51	52	53	54	55	56	57	58	59	60
61	62	63	64	65	66	67	68	69	70
71	72	73	74	75	76	77	78	79	80
81	82	83	84	85	86	87	88	89	90
91	92	93	94	95	96	97	98	99	100

FITNESS POINT CHART

_____

NAME

_____

PARENT'S SIGNATURE

_____

HOME ROOM TEACHER

_____

DATE TURNED IN

No Waste Above the Waist

School:	Shallotte Middle School
	225 Village Road
	Shallotte, NC 28459
Phone:	(910) 754-6882
Contributor:	Ron Champion

Program Objective

- to build upper body and shoulder girdle strength

Materials/Equipment Needed

- gymnasium or recreation area
- scooters
- beanbags
- tug-of-war ropes
- balloons
- volleyball net
- jump ropes
- dyna bands
- floor tape
- balls

Procedures and Teaching Strategies

- emphasize "personal best" not partner competition

Program Description

The focus of this activity is on developing upper body and shoulder girdle strength. Fitness testing has identified muscular strength and endurance as the area where students score the lowest. In order to focus on the improvement of upper body strength, it is necessary to look beyond the traditional exercises or activities. Implementing nontraditional activities which not only develop muscular strength and endurance but also foster greater participation and fun require careful planning. Planning activities that disguise the hard work of fitness development and emphasize fun and participation are of utmost importance.

The following activities combine muscular strength and endurance in high participation situations.

A. Crabs in the Canal

Number of Players: 25-30

Use cones, rope or floor tape to establish boundaries.

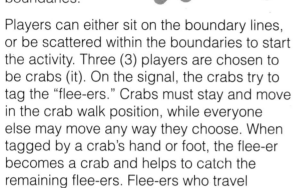

Players can either sit on the boundary lines, or be scattered within the boundaries to start the activity. Three (3) players are chosen to be crabs (it). On the signal, the crabs try to tag the "flee-ers." Crabs must stay and move in the crab walk position, while everyone else may move any way they choose. When tagged by a crab's hand or foot, the flee-er becomes a crab and helps to catch the remaining flee-ers. Flee-ers who travel outside the boundary automatically become crabs. All players must keep moving! Caution students not to grab or trip!

Variation: Snakes in the Grass

This game is basically the same except the "snakes" lie on their stomach and use only their arms and elbows to move around.

B. Station Activities

Tug-of-War: Students stand facing their partners, holding the rope between them. On the count of three (3), they begin trying to pull their partner over the line. They then try from a sitting position, and the third time they try from a kneeling position.

Push-Up – Put Back: Place two (2) beanbags on a bench or chair. The students assume a push-up position in front of the beanbags. Beginning with either hand, they remove one bag, place it on the floor, and do the same with the other hand. Repeat in reverse order. Partners challenge each other for the allotted time to see who can do the most – or they challenge themselves for a personal best.

Scooter Obstacle Course: Students must go through the cones in a figure eight fashion using **only** their arms. First, they go through forward; the second time, backwards; and the third time, using only their non-dominant hand.

Dyna Band Pull: Pull the bands in different directions and at different levels using arms and/or legs – above the head, in back, in front. Be creative! Have partners challenge each other to come up with different ways to work out with the bands.

Jump Rope: Practice each of the following rope tricks: alternate side-by-side, side-by-side, opposite side-by-side, and backward side-by-side. See if they can perform each one five (5) times.

Throw/Push-Ups: Partners face each other in a kneeling position. One partner tosses the ball and drops down and does a push-up. The other partner catches the ball, tosses it back and does a push-up. Play continues. Different weights of balls may be used as skill level improves.

Partner Push: Partners face each other standing on their line. With hands in an up position, they fall gently toward one another, catch and cooperatively push each other into an upright position. Lock hands and see how far they can walk apart and maintain balance, then walk back up.

Wall Push-Ups: Place tape on the floor away from the wall at the following intervals: 20 inches, 28 inches, and 36 inches. Players line up with heels on the first tape and lean forward to touch their nose to the wall. Heels must remain on the tape. They then push themselves back up into an upright position. Repeat 10-20 times, then rotate to the next tape. Repeat.

C. Crab Balloon Volley

Divide the class into two (2) teams. Place teams on opposite sides of a lowered volleyball net. Each team begins with six (6) inflated balloons. Balloons are put into play by members of the back line. The object of the game is to get all 12 balloons on one side. The team who does so is the winner. Balloons may be played by hands or feet, but team members **must** be in the crab walk position when they strike a balloon. A beach ball may be used with modified volleyball rules.

Program Results

Improved pull-up test scores by 10% in the first year.

Program Tips

Incorporate additional fitness education material into the activities such as pulse monitoring and upper body muscle location.

Physical Education for the 21st Century

School: Arthur E. Wright Middle School
              4029 N. Las Virgenes Road
              Calabasas, CA 91302
Phone: (818) 880-4614
Contributor: Jean R. Flemion–NASPE TEACHER OF THE YEAR
              Department Chair, Physical Education

Program Objectives

• to provide a success oriented program in a non-threatening environment

• to provide a coeducational non-traditional/experiential curriculum: (golf, fencing, self defense, dance, International Games, Circus Skills, Frisbee, Cooperative Games, hockey - floor and field, Olympics, Jogathon, Computerized Fitness Assessment, Personal Fitness Journals, Aerobic Homework, Cognitive lessons - personal fitness, athletic injuries - prevention and care, nutrition, consumer ed., social skills, and much more)

• to promote optimal growth in each individual:
  a. physical activity
  b. physical fitness and wellness
  c. movement skills and movement knowledge
  d. social development and interaction
  e. self-image and self-realization
  f. individual excellence

Materials/Equipment Needed

HEALTHY HEART NIGHT:

• gymnasium

• booths for testing/measurement

• equipment for testing/measurement

• stamps for each booth

• volunteers/staff/students to run the various stations

• skit/videos, posters and pamphlets created by students

PUBLIC RELATIONS PROGRAM:

• printing source

Procedures and Teaching Strategies

- get students involved through activities such as aerobic homework, personal fitness logs, fitness tests project, etc.

- publish a newsletter to communicate on a regular basis with parents, staff, and the rest of the school district to let them know what the physical education department is doing - report on special events, intramurals, course offerings, etc.

- do cooperative projects with other departments, i.e. Reading JOGS Your Mind

- aggressive Public Relations program (monthly newsletter, program brochure, demonstration teams, parent-student handbook, family sports nights, family Healthy Heart Night, and frequent newspaper, and radio recognition)

Program Description

PROGRAM EXIT OUTCOMES

Students will be:

- **Inspired self-directed learners** who create and enhance a healthy and active lifestyle, and participate to the best of their abilities.

- **Caring participants** who show empathy, fairness and appreciation for the contributions and efforts of themselves and others.

- **Cooperative and adaptable problem solvers** who effectively and positively communicate with one another and take responsibility for individually and collectively meeting challenges.

- **Self-empowered individuals** who apply knowledge of the disciplines of motor learning, bio-mechanics and exercise physiology to the pursuit of life-long mental, physical and emotional health.

- **Self-assured human beings** who experience and develop a healthy sense of the true joy and success found in physical activity.

ADDITIONAL PROGRAM IDEAS

- NOTES FROM THE LOCKER ROOM is a **Physical Education Department Newsletter**. Topics might include a report on *Jump Rope For Heart*, *Intramural Action*, *What Is Your Child Doing?* - tells which activities are currently taking place and gives information about the upcoming units.

- **Personal Fitness Journal** - students track their fitness experiences to help build a solid foundation for lifetime fitness habits.

- **Fitness Homework** - provides fitness opportunities and motivation during non-school hours.

- **Fitness Tests Project** - group interaction to learn about components of fitness and health.

- **Healthy Heart Night** - an evening dedicated to teaching parents, community and staff about the many aspects of a healthy heart. Displays and presentations by the physical education classes offer an exciting and fun filled evening.

TIP: The fitness journal presents an interdisciplinary opportunity to combine English with physical education by requiring students to write complete sentences in their journals.

MY PERSONAL FITNESS JOURNAL

DATE _____   ACTIVITY _____

SCORE: _____1. Yuk!   _____2. I Tried!   _____3. OK   _____4. Getting There!   _____5. Great!

Write two sentences describing your feelings about your performance in today's fitness activity.

_____

_____

DATE _____   ACTIVITY _____

SCORE: _____1. Yuk!   _____2. I Tried!   _____3. OK   _____4. Getting There!   _____5. Great!

Write two sentences describing your feelings about your performance in today's fitness activity.

_____

_____

DATE _____   ACTIVITY _____

SCORE: _____1. Yuk!   _____2. I Tried!   _____3. OK   _____4. Getting There!   _____5. Great!

Write two sentences describing your feelings about your performance in today's fitness activity.

_____

_____

DATE _____   ACTIVITY _____

SCORE: _____1. Yuk!   _____2. I Tried!   _____3. OK   _____4. Getting There!   _____5. Great!

Write two sentences describing your feelings about your performance in today's fitness activity.

_____

_____

DATE _____   ACTIVITY _____

SCORE: _____1. Yuk!   _____2. I Tried!   _____3. OK   _____4. Getting There!   _____5. Great!

Write two sentences describing your feelings about your performance in today's fitness activity.

_____

_____

TIP: When reproducing for classroom handouts, copy pages 60 and 61 back to back.

THE FITNESS HOME CHART

DIRECTIONS: This special physical fitness program is designed to improve your aerobic fitness and make your heart and lungs stronger. Select one of the activities listed below. The selected activity should be performed continuously for the time indicated. You earn 2 points if you perform the activity after school hours, and 3 points if you complete the number of minutes indicated. Record your progress on the Fitness Point Chart.

BE PROUD OF YOURSELF

Have your parents sign the chart—turn it in for credit.

ACTIVITY	# OF MINUTES
WALKING (FAST)	15
JOGGING	10
ROPE JUMPING	7
BICYCLE RIDING	20
SWIMMING	15
SOCCER	20
BASKETBALL	20
AEROBICS	15
OTHER	

- While many activities such as softball, bowling, and golf are fun to do, they were not included on the chart because they are not continuous aerobic activities.

- If you have questions on other activities, please ask.

TIP: When reproducing for classroom handouts, copy pages 60 and 61 back to back.

FITNESS POINT CHART

1	2	3	4	5	6	7	8	9	10
11	12	13	14	15	16	17	18	19	20
21	22	23	24	25	26	27	28	29	30
31	32	33	34	35	36	37	38	39	40
41	42	43	44	45	46	47	48	49	50
51	52	53	54	55	56	57	58	59	60
61	62	63	64	65	66	67	68	69	70
71	72	73	74	75	76	77	78	79	80
81	82	83	84	85	86	87	88	89	90
91	92	93	94	95	96	97	98	99	100
101	102	103	104	105	106	107	108	109	110

NAME: _____

PARENT'S SIGNATURE: _____

HOME ROOM TEACHER: _____

DATE TURNED IN: _____

TIP: When reproducing for classroom handouts, copy pages 62 and 63 back to back.

FITNESS HOMEWORK

A — Cardiovascular	B — Muscular Endurance	C — Strength	D — Flexibility	E — Recreational	F — Family Activities	G — Team Sports
Run 6 hrs	800 sit-ups / 100 push-ups	Run 1 hr / Weight training 1 hr	6 hrs yoga	Racquetball 8 hrs	Bring family ideas to your teacher to determine point value for activities. *2 bonus points for doing Fitness Homework with a family member.	Hockey / Soccer / Football / Basketball — 6 hrs
Run 5 hrs	Weight training 2 hrs			Tennis 10 hrs		
Run 4 hrs				Hike 3 days		
Run 3 hrs	Run 1 hr / 200 Sit-ups / 100 Push-ups	200 push-ups each of the 3 positions		Basketball 8 hrs		
Run 2 hrs				Dance 6 hrs		Volleyball / Softball — 12 hrs
Run 1 hr	Stationary bike 3 hrs		6 hrs stretching	Surf 9 hrs		
Bike 6 hrs	Jumping rope 1 hr / Stationary bike 2 hrs	150 pull-ups or pull-downs	Arms / Shoulders / Lower back / Legs / Ankles / Neck	Alpine ski 4 days / X-Cntry ski 2 days		
Walk 2 hrs / Run/Walk 1 hr				Swim 6 hrs / Kayaking 7 hrs / Rowing 7 hrs		
Bike 2 hrs / Walk 1 hr	Jumping rope 1 hr / 50 pull-ups/downs / 50 Dips			See teacher		
Walk .5 hr						

TIP: When reproducing for classroom handouts, copy pages 62 and 63 back to back.

FITNESS HOMEWORK

NAME _____   PERIOD _____

Points	Month	A-G Category	Activity	Parent Signature

TIP: When reproducing for classroom handouts, copy pages 64 and 65 back to back.

READING **JOGS** YOUR MIND
MARATHON

READY...SET...GO FOR THE FINISH LINE!

The library and the Physical Education Department invite you to put your best foot forward to meet the challenge of a reading/running marathon. Read, run and exercise for FUN AND PRIZES.

ENTER

Fill out the OFFICIAL GAMEBOARD entry form on the next page.
Keep it with you in your ring binder in order to mark your progress along the course.

RULES

Keep the log of reading and exercise activities below verified and up to date.
This will be checked on the following dates:

10K: _____   1/2 MARATHON: _____

THE WALL: _____   FINISH LINE! _____

VERIFICATION

Reading must be verified by your teacher, a librarian, or a parent. Exercise must be verified by your Physical Education teacher or a parent.

READING/EXERCISE LOG

1. Read for 1/2 hour _____

2. Skip rope 10 minutes _____

3. Read for 1/2 hour _____

4. Perimeter Run _____

Congratulations! You've completed the 10K!

5. Check out a book from the library _____

6. Walk 30 minutes with a family member _____

7. Read for 1/2 hour _____

8. Run, bike, or swim 30 minutes and/or read for one hour _____

9. Read to someone for 20 minutes _____

10. Run a mile _____

11. Read 10 poems _____

Great! You've made it through the 1/2 marathon.

12. Rollerblade, hike, dance, do aerobics, ski (1 hour) _____

13. Read for 1/2 hour _____

14. Do 50 jumping jacks, 50 sit-ups, 50 push-ups _____

Fantastic! You've hit the wall. Almost done!!

15. Read for one hour _____

16. Skip rope with a partner (20 minutes) _____

17. Read a comic book or magazine (cover to cover) _____

18. Run, bike, or swim (30 minutes) and/or read for one hour _____

Hooray! You've finished the entire marathon!!!

TIP: When reproducing for classroom handouts, copy pages 64 and 65 back to back.

Name _____

Period _____

CHOOSE ONE

| DO 50 JUMPING JACKS 50 SIT-UPS 50 PUSH-UPS | READ FOR 1 HOUR | SKIP ROPE WITH A PARTNER 20 MINUTES | READ A COMIC BOOK OR MAGAZINE (COVER TO COVER) | RUN BIKE OR SWIM 30 MINUTES / READ FOR 1 HOUR | FINISH LINE |

CHOOSE ONE

READ FOR 1/2 HOUR

ROLLERBLADE HIKE DANCE DO AEROBICS FOR 1 HOUR

MARATHON

CHOOSE ONE

| READ 10 POEMS | RUN A MILE | READ TO SOMEONE FOR 20 MINUTES | RUN BIKE OR SWIM 30 MINUTES / READ FOR 1 HOUR | READ FOR 1/2 HOUR |

CHOOSE ONE

WALK WITH A FAMILY MEMBER

READING *JOGS* YOUR MIND!

CHECK OUT A BOOK FROM THE LIBRARY

| START | READ FOR 1/2 HOUR | SKIP ROPE 10 MINUTES | READ FOR 1/2 HOUR | PERIMETER RUN |

HEALTHY HEART NIGHT

Healthy Heart Night is the culminating activity for a 12-week health and heart education unit. The next seven pages are all interrelated activities of this easy-to-implement program. The activities are as flexible as you want to make them — the following sample handouts will give you ideas of what has worked well. This sample program was designed for and conducted by 7th graders, however, you could adjust the level of activities to suit younger or older age categories.

At the end of the 12-week study unit, the class/classes involved hold Healthy Heart Night where families are invited to participate in a host of events which are fun yet educational about the Heart. Included with handouts for Healthy Heart Night is an invitation the children can take home to invite parents (you could also send one to the local media), a worksheet that guides participants through a maze of Heart check points, and a certificate of completion to reward everyone who attends Healthy Heart Night.

There are many more ideas you'll come up with to promote and include at Healthy Heart Night. Check the introductory section of this manual for additional guidance in promoting fitness programs and special events.

TIP: When planning your Healthy Heart Night program, let parents and the local media know from the beginning what your classroom is doing, and invite their involvement.

TIP: When reproducing for classroom handouts, copy pages 67 and 68 back to back.

HEALTHY HEART PROJECT - 100 POINTS

Groups of four or five (see me about other arrangements)

Each group will choose one component of health or skill related fitness and three tests related to this component to investigate and report on. Explain the value of this component of fitness; explain why it is important to health/fitness. Describe each test, find out and report on established norms for that test; tell who might use this test and why; how might this test aid someone in evaluating their personal health and fitness. Last, list and describe activities/ exercises which can be done to improve this component of fitness.

Each group will earn one grade. Each group must choose one of the following to present their findings.

1. Pamphlet - Create an informative health pamphlet to be passed out on Healthy Heart Night, and to classmates. A presentation about the pamphlet must be made to the class.

2. Posters - Make a minimum of three full-sized posters (24" x 36" or larger) with information regarding your group topic to be displayed at Healthy Heart Night. Make a presentation to the class regarding your posters.

3. Skit/Video - Develop a skit or video about your group topic to be presented on Healthy Heart Night and to the class.

4. Comparative Research - Conduct your own research to compare with established norms/ "best"/minimum health standards for the three tests you are investigating.

5. Other - See me if you have other ideas.

Each group must have at least one representative at Healthy Heart Night. Students presenting at Healthy Heart Night will earn extra credit.

Healthy Heart Night : _____(DATE)_____

Project Due : _____

Names of group members:

_____

_____

_____

_____

_____

_____

_____

_____

_____

_____

TIP: When reproducing for classroom handouts, copy pages 67 and 68 back to back.

HEALTHY HEART PROJECT - 100 POINTS

POSTERS

Posters must be at least 24 inches by 36 inches. Quality of work is very important!

POINTS	POSTER #1
20	Describe, define the component of fitness. Explain the value of this component of fitness; explain why it is important to health and fitness.

POSTER #2

20	Describe/explain the three tests. Instructions/diagrams. Who might use this test and why? Norms/minimal health standards, what do the results mean, implications of results on personal health and/or performance ability.

POSTER #3

20	Activities/exercises to improve this area of fitness
15	Oral presentation to the class. (All group members present.)
15	Neatness, special effects, illustration, mechanics, creativity and added information. (5 points per poster)
10	A bibliography of references (minimum of 3) must be included on the back of one of the posters (library, teacher, or other pre-approved sources).

100 TOTAL POINTS

The posters may include magazine cut-outs, drawings, special effects and other creative and artistic endeavors that illustrate your points.

A rough draft must be presented for approval by_____.

Extra Credit: Extra work, extra creative, extra special to look at, extra poster, present at Healthy Heart Night.

TIP: When reproducing for classroom handouts, copy pages 69 and 70 back to back.

HEALTHY HEART PROJECT - 100 POINTS
PAMPHLET

POINTS   PAGE/COMPONENT

10   ONE–Title page: Title of topic/pamphlet, members of group, period, teacher, date. Eye catching titles/artwork.

15   TWO–Describe, define the component of fitness. Explain the value of this component of fitness; explain why it is important to health and fitness.

15   THREE–Describe/explain the three tests. Instructions/ diagrams; who might use this test and why.

15   FOUR–Norms/minimal health standards, what do the results mean, implications of results on personal health and/or performance ability.

15   FIVE–Activities/exercises to improve this area of fitness.

10   SIX–References (Bibliography format)

10   NEATNESS/READABILITY–Look of the final pamphlet, easy to read, informative, error free.

10   CLASS PRESENTATION–Present and explain pamphlet to the class. (All group members must be present.)

100 TOTAL POINTS

On a note card, provide names of people in group and page assignments.

You must conduct library/reference research on your topic (books, magazines, periodicals, interviews, etc.).

All pamphlets must be typed/computerized.

Teacher will assist in assembly and run-off of pamphlet for the group.

Rough draft must be turned in by _____ for approval.

Final copy must be turned in for duplication by _____

TIP: When reproducing for classroom handouts, copy pages 69 and 70 back to back.

HEALTHY HEART PROJECT - 100 POINTS
SKIT OR VIDEO

POINTS	PAGE/COMPONENT
5	Title of skit/video.
5	Actors involved (cast and characters).
5	Definition of topic.
15	Script of who says what and what is to be done. Must be written in detail and turned in by _____ for approval **before** shooting your video.
10	Describe, define, and show the component of fitness. Explain the value of this component of fitness; explain why it is important to health and fitness.
10	Describe/explain and show the three tests. Instructions/diagrams. Who might use this test and why.
10	Norms/minimal health standards, what do the results mean, implications of results on personal health and/or performance ability.
10	Activities/exercises to improve this area of fitness.
10	Ending Credits (references–tv, radio, class discussions, magazines, newspapers, books, interviews with fitness instructors, famous athletes or trainers, etc.)
10	Time limit 5-10 minutes. All must have equal work/performance.
10	Speech/performance (lines memorized; eye contact; prepared; speak loud, slow and clear)

100 TOTAL POINTS

EXTRA CREDIT: Extra work, extra creative, props, costumes, music, present on Healthy Heart Night

YOUR PERSONAL INVITATION

Healthy

Heart

Night

_____

PLACE

_____

DATE

_____

TIME

TIP: Attendants at each station should fill the heart with red pencil, stamp or marker to indicate the participant has completed that station.

HEART NIGHT BOOTHS

1. Blood Pressure: Systolic_____   Diastolic_____

2. Cardiovascular: RHR_____   MHR_____   THR_____

3. Cardiorespiratory Endurance: (step test)
Exercise Heart Rate _____   Recovery Heart Rate _____

4. Flexibility: sit & reach _____

5. Body Composition (measurements): Total Score _____% Body Fat_____

6. Balance: hop on line _____

7. Speed and Power: long jump _____   vertical jump_____

8. Agility and Coordination: shuttle run _____   side step_____

9. Muscle Strength: pull-ups/modified pull-ups (upper body) _____

10. Muscular Endurance: sit-ups (abdominal) _____

11. Heart and Exercise: List one way exercise benefits the heart:

_____

12. Lungs and Exercise: List one way exercise benefits the lungs:

_____

13. Nutrition: What is the recommended daily caloric intake of food per day for your age? _____

14. Sports Injury Prevention:
R_____   I_____   C_____   E_____

15. F_____   I_____   T_____

16. F = How_____   I = How_____
                    T = How_____

17. Stress: (questionnaire)

Certificate of Completion and Appreciation

This signifies that _____

has completed all the events at

"Healthy Heart Night"

_____
DATE

ULTRA-SHUFFLE

School: Tilford Middle School
308 East 13th St.
Vinton, IA 52349
Phone: (319) 472-4736
Contributor: Beth Kirkpatrick–NASPE TEACHER OF THE YEAR

Program Objectives

- to provide a non-threatening environment for sports and games

- to introduce a system to handle large numbers of students and situations where class size varies day to day

- to provide an effective organizational system for the middle school physical education curriculum

- to encourage students to challenge themselves

- to teach students that they are only keeping score for themselves

Materials/Equipment Needed

- jerseys/pinnies

- plastic cones

- referee jerseys

- whistles

Procedures and Teaching Strategies

- everyone will experience the need for acceptance as they come and go during the ULTRA-SHUFFLE

- acceptance becomes a personal experience

- emphasis is on playing rather than winning

Program Description

At Tilford Middle School the ULTRA-SHUFFLE is used during the 20 minute activity period within the physical education class. Activities leading up to the ULTRA-SHUFFLE include stretching and aerobic conditioning. The 20 minute activity period is used to concentrate on a particular sport or carry-over activity throughout a two (2) - four (4) week unit. All units include lead-up skills and modified games during the first half of the unit. The remaining half of the unit is used for actual game participation. This is where the ULTRA-SHUFFLE proves most useful.

The ULTRA-SHUFFLE is a system, in operation all game days, which combines individual skills development, random team selections, unlimited team combinations that change throughout the activity time, one-on-one instructor help (without losing class management effectiveness), student referees who interchange with participants, fitness testing that does not interfere with activities, class time efficiency, total participation, multiple game situations where scores are not kept, and win/loss outcomes that are never recognized—usually undetermined.

The ULTRA-SHUFFLE can be used in any individual, partner, or team activity with virtually any number of participants. It works equally well indoors or outdoors.

How to Perform the ULTRA-SHUFFLE

Step 1 : Determine sport to be played.

Example: Basketball

Step 2 : Determine number of team members of the selected sport.

Example: Basketball has five (5) players.

Step 3: Multiply number of team members by two (2).

Example: Five (5) x two (2) = ten (10)

Step 4: Equally assign students to ten (10) rows.

Example: If you had 70 students, it would look like this.

ROW	1 —	2 —	3 —	4 —	5 —	6 —	7 —	8 —	9 —	10
PARTICIPANTS	1	2	3	4	5	6	7	8	9	10
	1	2	3	4	5	6	7	8	9	10
	1	2	3	4	5	6	7	8	9	10
	1	2	3	4	5	6	7	8	9	10
	1	2	3	4	5	6	7	8	9	10
	1	2	3	4	5	6	7	8	9	10
	1	2	3	4	5	6	7	8	9	10

Step 5: A marker of some kind (plastic cone) is placed in front of each row. Draped over the cone is a jersey/pinnie of the color each member of that row is to wear. Directly behind that cone will be the rest of the jerseys/pinnies of that color in a box. There should be enough jerseys/pinnies for all students assigned to that row to wear.

Example: To play five (5) on five (5) basketball, there would be five (5) rows with blue jerseys and five (5) rows with red jerseys.

ROW	1	2	3	4	5	6	7	8	9	10
PARTICIPANTS	R	R	R	R	R	B	B	B	B	B
	R	R	R	R	R	B	B	B	B	B
	R	R	R	R	R	B	B	B	B	B
	R	R	R	R	R	B	B	B	B	B
	R	R	R	R	R	B	B	B	B	B
	R	R	R	R	R	B	B	B	B	B
	R	R	R	R	R	B	B	B	B	B

KEY: R = red jersey   B = blue jersey

The instructor will determine which half of the rows wear the blue jerseys one day and which half wear red. This will change every class. You can choose any combination of rows, but the important idea is to change on a regular basis.

Step 6: Each row of blue and red jerseys will have a different symbol, one that is unique to that row only. These symbols can be numbers or letters or shapes. This symbol will be displayed only on the front of the jersey. Example: Using numbers, the numbers 1-5 could be on the red jerseys, and the numbers 6-10 could be on the blue jerseys. All students in the row need to have the same color jersey <u>with</u> the same number on the front.

ROW	1 — 2 — 3 — 4 — 5 — 6 — 7 — 8 — 9 —10									
	R4	B6	R2	B7	R1	B8	R3	B10	R5	B9
	R4	B6	R2	B7	R1	B8	R3	B10	R5	B9
	R4	B6	R2	B7	R1	B8	R3	B10	R5	B9
PARTICIPANTS	R4	B6	R2	B7	R1	B8	R3	B10	R5	B9
	R4	B6	R2	B7	R1	B8	R3	B10	R5	B9
	R4	B6	R2	B7	R1	B8	R3	B10	R5	B9
	R4	B6	R2	B7	R1	B8	R3	B10	R5	B9

Key: R4 = red jersey with a number 4 on it
B8 = blue jersey with an 8 on it

<u>Note:</u> Each student will be assigned to a particular row for the duration of the nine weeks. Once the individual has been assigned to that row, he/she will be in that row every session. Once the students have learned this system, they are able to quickly get the proper color jersey with the correct symbol on and assemble in their respective rows without any instructions.

Five (5) ULTRA-SHUFFLE Rules:

1) Students must substitute for only those students who have the SAME COLOR JERSEY AND THE SAME NUMBER (blue 7).

2) No individual may return to the same game he/she was taken out of.

3) Once a student has been signaled for substitution, they must leave without hesitation.

4) To return to the games, a student must complete the assigned "task of the day" at the designated area.

5) Before a student enters a game, they must turn their jersey around so that the number is on the back (all numbers begin on the front) to signify that they have already been out once.

Students can not be taken out more than once until all students with the same color and same number have been out once. After all students have been out, the next rotation will be with the referees. Students will begin the second rotation by turning their jerseys back to the front. Games do not stop for substitutions.

Beginning the ULTRA-SHUFFLE

Step 1: Students will assemble behind their assigned cones immediately putting on their respective jerseys and waiting for the instructions.

Step 2: Teams are determined at the beginning of the activity time with the instructor announcing court assignments according to the class size. For a class of 70 students during a basketball unit, there would be ten (10) rows of seven (7) students per row. To allow for skill development and referee experience, there would be five game situations simultaneously in progress with one area open for "task of the day" at a side basket. Within a gymnasium, the five games could be played at side baskets using half court five on five rules.

Step 3: The instructor asks the first person in each of the ten rows to step forward. There will be five blues and five reds. They will be assigned to court number one (1). The game can begin immediately.

Step 4: The second person in each of the ten rows is now in the front. The instructor again asks for the first person in each row to step forward. There will be five blues and five reds. These two teams will go to court number two (2) and the game will begin immediately.

Step 5: The third person in each row is now at the front of the rows. The instructor will ask them to step forward. There will be five reds and five blues. The instructor can decide to send these ten players to the skill station. Before these students can enter the games, they will be asked to complete a "task of the day". One day, that task could be to ATTEMPT five right-handed lay-ups and five left-handed lay-ups. As soon as any or all of the students have completed this task, they are free to enter the game of their choice. Each game will have one person from each of their rows. Therefore, the person completing the task at the skill station has the right to enter any one of the games of his/her choice. The person who has been taken out by one of the students from the skill station will immediately go to the skill station and complete the task of attempting right and left hand lay-ups. This process continues throughout the remaining minutes of the class.

Step 6: The fourth person in each line will now be at the front of the row. The instructor again asks the first person to step forward in each line. There will be five blues and five reds. These two teams will be assigned to court number three (3).

Step 7: The fifth person in each line will now be the first person in the row. The instructor again asks the first person to step forward in each row. There will be five reds and five blues. These two teams will be assigned to court number four (4).

Step 8: The sixth person in each line will now be the first person in the row. The instructor again asks the first person to step forward. There will be five reds and five blues. The instructor assigns these ten people to begin the activity time as referees. They put on referee jerseys and pick up a clean whistle and go immediately to the games that are already in progress and referee until they are taken out during the shuffle.

Step 9: The seventh person in each line is now the only one left in each row. These five blues and five reds are assigned to court number five (5) and begin playing.

ALL GAMES AND PARTICIPANTS ARE NOW IN FULL ACTION WITH NO ONE SITTING OUT. CONSTANT CHANGE IS TAKING PLACE.

As substitutions enter and leave, time is not called. Teams are undergoing continual change randomly altering team members. Team members are being determined by neither the instructors nor the students exclusively. Nearly equal time is spent in participation, refereeing, and in skill development by all students.

Officiating

It is important to note that one person from each row is an official. Once the student has substituted as a game participant at each court, they must substitute as an official before they can repeat the cycle. No one is allowed to dispute, question, ask for an interpretation, or interfere with a referee's call. We respect his/her judgement, right or wrong, and recognize how difficult the job is. There is a need for all students to gain knowledge of the rules that are necessary for each activity and gain first hand experience as a referee using this knowledge. An appreciation for sportsmanship can sometimes only be understood through this experience. This is also an excellent exercise in developing assertiveness.

Key Teaching Objectives

Key teaching objectives are to develop self-confidence and encourage acceptance of oneself within all students. Everyone will experience the need for acceptance as they come and go during the ULTRA-SHUFFLE. They sense an understanding through this experience that they might not have received in any other way. As individuals participate in the ULTRA-SHUFFLE, acceptance becomes a personal experience. It becomes automatic to give acceptance and you learn to EXPECT to receive acceptance. Both of these important characteristics are needed for proper development in social and emotional health. The emphasis is on playing, rather than on winning. It is impossible to keep score using this system. The lifestyle teaching concept is to encourage students to challenge themselves, and for each student to realize that they are keeping score for themselves. Artificial scorekeepers such as coaches, parents, teachers, or friends should not be the judge on personal successes. Teaching students to base goals on personal expectations and outcomes brings self-respect for those accomplishments. A scoreboard is a poor substitute for this learning experience.

Program Options

- Nearly every game can be played with three (3) or four (4) team members. Keeping the teams small encourages each participant to be an active member.

- The skill station could be used for fitness testing.

- The skill station could be used as a cognitive station with written worksheets to be filled in with information about the sport or skill being studied, i.e. scoring, rules, equipment, strategy, safety.

Part II

High School Program Ideas

Assessment Ideas for Physical Education

School: Health Careers Academy
Bell Gardens High School
6119 Agra Street
Bell Gardens, CA 90201
Phone: (213) 773-3871
Contributor: Carolyn Thompson–NASPE NATIONAL TEACHER OF THE YEAR

Program Objectives

- to give students a better understanding of why physical education is taught in the school curriculum

- to define relationships between social skills and physical education

- to apply biomechanical principles when learning new activities

Materials/Equipment Needed

- library

- poster paper

- gymnasium (or recreation area)

- sports equipment (balls, nets, etc.)

- video tape and camera

- Textbook:
  <u>Moving for Life</u>, by Gary B. Spindt, William H. Monti and Betty Hennessy, Ph.D. (Dubuque, IA: Kendall/Hunt Publishing Company 1991)

Procedures and Teaching Strategies

- use a multitude of disciplines to better understand the role physical education has played in history and how it continues to affect many different dimensions in our lives

Program Description

The following programs are designed to give three different approaches to the question of why physical education is important in the school curriculum and what students get out of it that can help them for a lifetime.

I. A HISTORICAL PERSPECTIVE OF PHYSICAL EDUCATION

Knowledge of how past experiences have influenced the present can help students to recognize the importance of preparing today to meet the goals they have set for themselves in the future.

Project: Have students research the history of physical education. Study groups of four (4) can be formed by the students according to interest. The time in history can range from Ancient Greece to the present.

- Ancient Greece
    Athens
    Sparta

- Ancient Olympic Games

- Ball Games in Ancient Greece

- Sport and Physical Education in the Middle Ages

- Sport and Physical Education During the Renaissance

- Nineteenth Century Influences on Sport and Physical Education

- The Colonial Period to 1900

- 1900's to 1920's

- 1920's to 1940's

- 1940's to 1980's

- 1980's to present

- Historical Development of the Physical Fitness Movement
    Period of World War I
    Period of World War II
    Postwar Education and Improvement of Fitness
    Lifetime Sports Movement
    Physical Education and Medicine
    The U.S. Government, Conferences, and the President's Council on Physical Fitness and Sports
    Trends and Needs

Other time frames and topics can be added. For example, one class researched Ancient Greece up to the Nineteenth Century Influences while another class worked from the Colonial Period to the present including Physical Fitness Movement.

The assignment included four (4) areas of research, one for each member of the team. The students went to the library for a full period of physical education. Each team collaborated content, dates and information in their interest area. From their notes, they designed how to lay out their time lines. Each study group worked with their own poster paper to show the education, physical education, medicine, and politics occurring during that time in history. A title, the dates, many pictures and drawings, and brief descriptions began to unfold the history of physical education.

Each member of the team shall present their area of expertise. Hang the time lines in order of historical occurrence. Video tape the presentations and share with the other classes so a complete historical perspective is experienced by all the students.

The final product was assessed from a criteria sheet which each group received from the beginning of the project at the library (See Chart 1).

A follow-up project included writing a letter to the Board of Education in support of a fourth year of physical education in the school district. The letter's criteria included: a historical perspective, the value of physical education in the school's curriculum, how to make healthy choices, and the role of fitness in maintaining an active lifestyle.

Chart 1

Time line	15 pts.
Art work	10 pts.
Descriptions	15 pts.
Education	10 pts.
Physical Education	10 pts.
Medicine	10 pts.
Politics	10 pts.
Presentation skills	
Speak clearly	5 pts.
Speak slowly	5 pts.
Speak loudly	5 pts.
Transition with team members	5 pts.
Total points	**100 pts.**

II. SOCIAL SKILLS

Students are asked to select adjectives which describe their personality. They "pair share" why they selected each word. On the board, common adjectives and non-similar adjectives are listed. After these skills are introduced through discussion, five (5) or more adjectives are selected by the students for a social behavior project.
For example:

• kindness

• thoughtful

• encourage

• respect

• honesty

Have each student define the word with a partner. The pair partners write a definition and describe how the behavior is used during a physical education class as well as in their daily life outside of school. It is important that students are able to make the link of how the use of physical skills interrelate with social skills. The students' homework is to implement each word. This is the performance of the task. One word a day or a week can be discussed in class and performed. The students are given time to process the social skill and discover how it changed their social behavior. Pair partners answer such questions as: What did it feel like when you performed the social behavior? How did the recipient of the behavior react or feel?

An initiative activity is used to begin class. This warms the group up with laughter, communication, collaboration, trust and fun. It allows for social skills to be practiced in a physical environment. The teachers' learning expectations are seen in the social behavior of the students as well.

Social Behavior Chart							
BEHAVIOR	**S**	**M**	**T**	**W**	**T**	**F**	**S**
KINDNESS							
THOUGHTFUL							
ENCOURAGE							
RESPECT							
HONESTY							

NAME   PERIOD

Respect is a definite outcome for student to student, teacher to student, and student to teacher.

A social behavior chart can be designed so each word is listed going down the left hand column and the dates of use are written across the top of the chart. Each paper has the group's name and period of physical education. This chart now becomes a part of the expected behavior in each unit.

The assessment is done by the students at the end of the period during the closure part of the lesson. This chart may lead to the use of graphs to show mood changes. Understanding became an additional word on the list. Students learned to accept individual differences. Attitude adjustment was identified and discussed. Such pair share questions including: How do I change my attitude toward people, toward physical activity, and/or toward my life?

III. MOVEMENT ANALYSIS THROUGH THE USE OF BIOMECHANICS

After studying biomechanic principles for six (6) weeks, the students select a sport they enjoy. Groups of four (4) are formed by selecting a specific skill within that sport. Each member of the group selects a task: performer, assistant performer, reader and video recorder.

A. The study group identifies the biomechanic principles which apply to their movement.

B. They then write out descriptions of the principles and where each applies in the movement.

C. Once the written documentary is completed, the group performs the movement.

D. Four (4) video cameras are acquired from the media center on campus so four (4) groups may record at one time. The other groups practice their presentation while waiting for the video camera. Three (3) groups are assigned to each camera.

E. Video taping includes the following tasks: one (1) student video tapes, one (1) student reads the documentary designed earlier by the group and two (2) students demonstrate and perform the movement pattern over and over again until the reader has completed the biomechanic analysis.

The students then turn in their video tape along with their analysis sheet. The teacher and the students view the video tape together to discuss appropriate and inappropriate biomechanic analysis.

Biomechanic Analysis Criteria Sheet

Name _____ Name _____

Name _____ Name _____

PRINCIPLE	POSSIBLE POINTS	EARNED POINTS	COMMENTS
Skeletal System	5		
(Joints)			
Muscular System	5		
Newton's First Law	5		
Newton's Second Law	5		
Newton's Third Law	5		
Force	5		
Types of Motion	5		
Levers	5		
Projectiles	5		
Spin and Rebound	5		
Force Absorption	5		
Presentation	10		
Narrator			
Video			
TOTAL POINTS	**65**		

GRADING SCALE

65-58 **A**   57-52 **B**   51-45 **C**   44-39 **D**   38-32 **F**

Program Results

All of the programs involved a multi-discipline approach to learning about physical education and the role it has played in history and continues to play in the students' lives.

Students looked at physical education in another light after researching its historical perspective.

In the social skills project, students became counselors to one another. Caring and sharing had occurred!

Movements which students had taken for granted all their lives were appreciated more after the movement analysis.

Program Tips

Share results from these programs with other classes in the physical education program.

Challenge students to come up with creative ideas to utilize in their physical education programming. This develops ownership in the program along with increased enthusiasm.

BodyWorks

School: Highland Park High School
433 Vine Avenue
Highland Park, IL 60035
Phone: (708) 926-9231
Contributor: Bonnie S. Voss–NASPE TEACHER OF THE YEAR

Program Objectives

- to provide knowledge, understanding, and raise performance levels in the components of health related fitness

- to set the groundwork for a lifetime commitment to fitness

Materials/Equipment Needed

- physical education instructor/fitness dance background

- gymnasium (or recreation area)

- classroom setting

- proper flooring for fitness dance activity

- jump ropes, hand weights, elastic resistance tubing/bands, towels, wands, bench for stepping activity

- fitness assessment equipment

Procedures and Teaching Strategies

- introduce a new activity each week to continually challenge and motivate students

- use a combination of activities to expose students to multiple choices in their search for lifetime exercise

- relate classroom time directly to activity sessions in order to teach and demonstrate course content on a personal level

Program Description

BodyWorks can be incorporated as a departmental offering in the high school Physical Education department. Course descriptions follow.

BodyWorks 1-2

This full year course for juniors and seniors highlights fitness routines that combine low and high impact aerobics, hand weights, weight training, bench stepping, and elastic resistance equipment (power cords, bands, and tubing). Other activities include power walking, nutrition sessions, stress management, pulse awareness, injury prevention, and body alignment.

BodyWorks 2-3

This advanced course challenges experienced fitness students with more intricate routines performed at higher target zones, power sculpting with heavier weights, and the use of increasingly more difficult resistance equipment. Advanced students have the opportunity to train as fitness instructors. The prerequisite for this course is successful completion of BodyWorks 1-2.

I. COURSE PURPOSE

Research tells us that adequate exercise will develop an efficient and effective cardiovascular system, a certain degree of muscular strength and endurance, and ample flexibility. These components of health-related fitness combined with controlled body weight, good nutrition, and reduced levels of stress, help prevent disabilities and disease and promote an effective, functional lifestyle.

The purpose of this course is to provide knowledge, understanding, and raise performance levels in the six components of health-related fitness as well as the realization that this means lifetime commitment.

The components of HRF:

1. Cardiovascular efficiency
2. Muscular strength and endurance
3. Flexibility
4. Weight control
5. Nutrition
6. Stress Reduction

II. PERFORMANCE OBJECTIVES AND COURSE CONTENT

Performance Objectives

- To develop heightened self-awareness and increase self-confidence

- Increase muscle strength, flexibility, and endurance

- Understand basic anatomical and physiological terminology

- Gain an understanding of nutrition and weight control concepts

- How basic components of fitness relate to individual lifestyle choices

- Gain knowledge of lifelong fitness needs

- Understand body composition

- Learn to set and evaluate personal fitness goals including relaxation and stress management

- Develop proper techniques and alignment for safe, injury-free participation in all fitness activities

II. PERFORMANCE OBJECTIVES AND COURSE CONTENT (cont.)

Course Content

- Combination impact (hi/low) aerobic dance routines and plyometrics
- Hand-held weight training
- Resistance training with power cords, bands and exercise tubing
- Power walking
- Bench-stepping
- Circuit training
- Lecture/Discussion on:
  - pulse monitoring
  - nutritional concepts
  - anatomical knowledge
  - injury prevention
  - body composition
  - stress management

III. COURSE OUTLINE
(*Introduction of New Activity Every Week)

A. First Quarter

Week 1

- Discuss proper workout gear (shoes & clothing)
- Review curriculum, components of fitness, class and individual goals and class format
- Terminology (glossary of fitness/dance definitions)
- Administer self-assessment tests to determine and monitor individual fitness levels
* Introduce basic low impact aerobic steps

Week 2

- Review important terms such as frequency, intensity, time, aerobic, and anaerobic
- Discuss Target Workout Zone and pulse monitoring, low impact routines with warm-up, stretch, progressive aerobic phase, and cool down
- Practice heart rate monitoring
- Terminology of basic cueing methods
* Introduce proper stretching techniques

Week 3

- Review cueing and pulse monitoring
- Proper techniques of posture and alignment
- Basic dance techniques of jazz, modern, and ballet and incorporating them into low impact routines
* Introduce power walking

Week 4

- Continue power walking
- Practice and review pulse monitoring
- Introduce new patterns into low impact routines stressing correctness of posture and alignment techniques
- Introduce correct belly breathing techniques
* Introduce strength and toning floor work

Week 5

- Review stretching and breathing techniques
- Add high impact steps to aerobic routines
- Review power walking skills
* Introduce hand held weight training with 1 lb. weights

Week 6

- Continue with toning floor work emphasizing abdominals
- Increase combo impact (high and low) work load
- Discuss prevention of most common aerobic injuries
* Introduce jump rope activities and use of circuit training in future

Week 7

- Incorporate running into aerobic routines
- Incorporate barre work into placement and toning work
- Increase distance of power walking
- Begin learning the major muscle groups and how to train for strength
- Perform hand held weight medley routines
* Introduce elastic resistance training with use of power cords, bands, and tubing

Week 8

- Continue injury prevention work with discussion and demonstration of correct/incorrect techniques, safe class procedures, and exercises to avoid
- Incorporate use of the wall into stretching and strength training
- Incorporate use of towels into stretching techniques
- Review and introduce more skills for elastic resistance training
* Introduce balancing skills with the use of wands

Week 9

- Fitness Monitoring Week, including written quiz and self-assessments in pulse monitoring, power walking, stretching, and strength/toning skills

B. Second Quarter

Second quarter will begin with a lecture/discussion on the subject of body composition and administration of a body composition test. For the remainder of the quarter, weekly workout sessions will be arranged to include the following:

- Two Days: aerobic activity including power walking (weather permitting), combo impact aerobic dance, and bench stepping (*new activity)

- Two Days: strength activity including 2 lb. hand held weights medley training, floor toning, and elastic resistance exercises.

- One Day: lesson devoted to one of the following subjects: weight control, nutrition, or stress reduction

* New activities introduced during the second quarter include bench stepping, plyometrics, relaxation techniques, and the beginning basics of yoga and Tai Chi. The basics of good nutrition and how it relates to overall health and optimum athletic performance will also be included this quarter.

SECOND SEMESTER P.E. FITNESS DANCE

C. Third Quarter

Third Quarter will begin with a review of the six health-related fitness components covered during first semester:
  1. Cardiovascular efficiency
  2. Muscular strength and endurance
  3. Flexibility
  4. Weight control
  5. Nutrition
  6. Stress Reduction

When this review is completed, lessons will be broken down into an in-depth study of each major muscle group in the body, including the cardiovascular system. As an example, identify all major muscles of the back, explicit exercises for strengthening and relaxing these muscles, and how to avoid injury to the area. Muscle groups will include shoulders, arms, chest, back, abdominals, gluteals, quads, hamstrings, neck, wrist, and ankles.

* New activities will include power sculpting with 3 lb. weights, partner work for both strength and flexibility, combining weight lifting with bench stepping, and the use of circuit training to increase cardiovascular endurance. During aerobic dance sessions, new rhythms and dance forms such as "funky," salsa, western, blues, and big band will be explored.

D. Fourth Quarter

Fourth Quarter will begin with administering the second body composition test, making comparisons and reevaluating personal fitness goals. In conjunction with this activity, the nutritional subjects of nutrients, balanced diets, special needs, cholesterol, ineffective weight-loss techniques, and eating disorders will be discussed. Discussion will be devoted to dispelling myths and misconceptions and how to make individual decisions for leading a healthful lifestyle. There will also be a review of current videos on the market and what to look for when choosing a health club or aerobics class.

Activities will include a return to outdoor power walking, bench stepping with weights, advanced aerobic routines, power sculpting with 4 lb. weights, elastic resistance training, and circuit training.

Note: Progressions throughout the year include individual self-assessment tests at the end of each quarter, with ongoing fitness monitoring. The aerobic routines increase in frequency, intensity, and time with each quarter, and students move up a pound in weights with each quarter. In addition, two videos on the subjects of nutrition and exercise are shown each quarter.

P.E. FITNESS DANCE EQUIPMENT

- **Hand Held Weights:** In addition to standard exercises such as rows, curls, flys and presses, free weights can be used to "load" the chest for challenging abdominal work, or to "load" the lower body while working legs and buttocks in a standing position.

- **Elastic Resistance:** Many options are available for strength training using elastic resistance such as bands and tubing. This equipment accommodates for different fitness levels by varying the degrees of resistance as muscles are moved from short to long ranges of motion. Elastic resistance can be applied quite creatively for upper, middle, and lower body conditioning.

- **Towels:** Towels can be used in some of the same ways as elastic resistance. Some contractions may be isometric and others can be moved through a range of motions. Grasp the towel overhead and pull down with one arm to work the latissimus dorsi. Also, towels can be used for stretching. In a long sitting position, hook the towel over one foot, gently pull the towel until you can feel a stretch in the calf.

- **Stepping Bench:** This newest accessory offers much more than the cardiorespiratory benefit of aerobic stepping. Used as a platform, standing leg and buttock work can be executed. From a seated position, quadricep extensions can be performed. Upper body work on the bench may include: incline and decline push-ups, tricep dips, pectoralis, and latissimus work. With one knee on the bench and the opposite foot on the floor, rows or side arm raises may be executed. Abdominal curl combinations with both knees bent and feet resting on the bench can be performed. Finally, several stretch variations are possible.

- **Jump Ropes:** Ropes are used for aerobic training. They can be incorporated into a group class for setting up a circuit which alternates the aerobic equipment with strength stations.

- **Wands:** Long wands can be used for balance during standing leg and gluteal work. Also wands can provide a "hookup" for elastic bands. Wands can enhance partner work and stretching efforts as well.

- **Walls:** They can be used for a variety of calisthenics or stretching positions such as wall push-ups, calf stretches, chair dips, and sitting stretches.

Program Tips

Topics to include in a course like this can be selected based on available equipment, expertise, and interest of students. A key point to remember is to continually offer new and innovative fitness activities.

Guest instructors can cover topic areas unfamiliar to the physical education professional. These instructors could be professionals in dance, athletic training, martial arts, nutrition, weight training, etc.

S A M P L E

Individual Fitness Goal Sheet

Short Range: to be achieved by the end of this class

1. _____
   _____

2. _____
   _____

3. _____
   _____

4. _____
   _____

5. _____
   _____

Long Range: to be achieved one (1) year from now

1. _____
   _____

2. _____
   _____

3. _____
   _____

4. _____
   _____

5. _____
   _____

SAMPLE

EXERCISE PRESCRIPTION FOR: _____

Date Started:_____

Mode	Monday	Tuesday	Wednesday	Thursday	Friday	Sat/Sun
Warm-Up						
Aerobic						
Strength						
Cool-Down Flexibility						

Progression Goals:

_____

_____

_____

_____

_____

Retest Date:

Comments:

_____

_____

_____

_____

SAMPLE

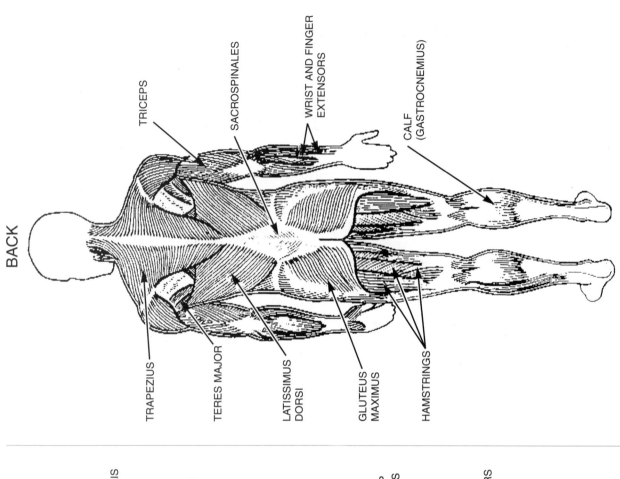

BACK

TRICEPS

SACROSPINALES

WRIST AND FINGER EXTENSORS

CALF (GASTROCNEMIUS)

TRAPEZIUS

TERES MAJOR

LATISSIMUS DORSI

GLUTEUS MAXIMUS

HAMSTRINGS

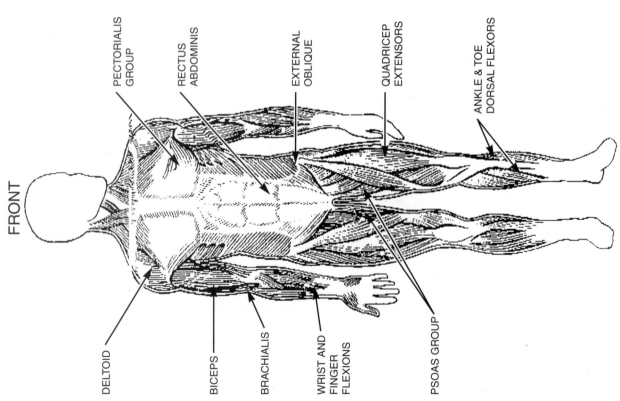

FRONT

PECTORIALIS GROUP

RECTUS ABDOMINIS

EXTERNAL OBLIQUE

QUADRICEP EXTENSORS

ANKLE & TOE DORSAL FLEXORS

DELTOID

BICEPS

BRACHIALIS

WRIST AND FINGER FLEXIONS

PSOAS GROUP

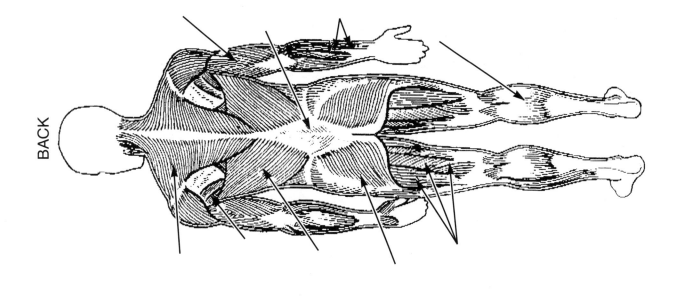

BACK

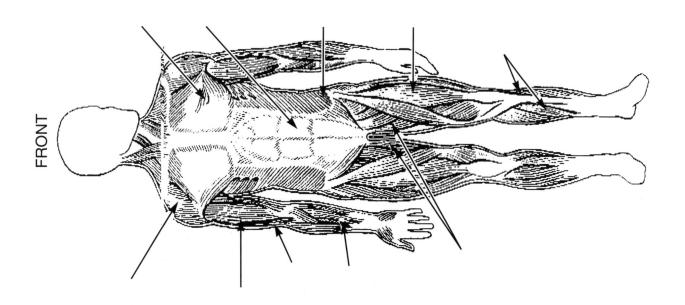

FRONT

Cardiovascular and Respiratory Systems During Exercise

School: Health Careers Academy
Bell Gardens High School
6119 Agra Street
Bell Gardens, CA 90201
Phone: (213) 773-3871
Contributor: Carolyn Thompson–NASPE NATIONAL TEACHER OF THE YEAR

Program Objectives

• to develop a working knowledge of what the cardiovascular and respiratory functions do during exercise

• to apply the FIT principles to the cardiovascular component of fitness

Materials/Equipment Needed

• 6' lengths of poster paper - one (1) per group of four (4) students

• one (1) black, red and blue marker per group of four (4) students

• scissors

• bottles of glue

• masking tape

• rubber bands

• Textbooks:
Fitness For Life, by Charles B. Corbin and Ruth Lindsey (Glenview, IL: Scott, Foresman and Company 1979).

Personal Fitness: Looking Good/Feeling Good, by Charles S. Williams, Emmanouel G. Harageones, DeWayne J. Johnson, and Charles D. Smith (Dubuque, IA: Kendall/Hunt Publishing Company 1986).

Moving For Life, by Gary B. Spindt, William H. Monti and Betty Hennessy, Ph.D. (Dubuque, IA: Kendall/Hunt Publishing Company 1991).

Basic Stuff Series I, by Pat Dodds, Editor (Reston, VA: American Alliance for Health, Physical Education, Recreation and Dance 1987).

Procedures and Teaching Strategies

• command, reciprocal, self check, and cooperative learning strategies are all utilized in this program

Program Description

This is a project for the cardiovascular component of fitness. The procedures listed below may take two (2) or more weeks depending upon the amount of time allotted the students to work on their posters. The work can be accomplished on the gym floor, the cafeteria, the library or in a classroom. Physical activity circuits were introduced each day which influenced the learning process and information to be included on the posters.

1. Form cooperative learning groups of four (4). Jigsaw reading assignment on cardiorespiratory system during exercise.

> Jigsaw is just one kind of cooperative learning strategy used to assist students in learning. The Jigsaw method allows a lot of content to be covered without having to read all of the material. The reading, the discussions, and the skill of reporting reinforces learning with meaning and understanding for the content.
>
> **EXAMPLE:**
> a. Assign each student in their home group of four a number #1, #2, #3, and #4.
> b. Assign each paragraph or concept to be read from the book with a number.
> > #1 Cardiovascular Fitness and Good Health, pg. 25
> > #2 Who Needs Cardiovascular Fitness, pg. 26
> > #3 Cardiovascular and Respiratory Systems, pg. 26
> > #4 Effects of Exercise on Cardiovascular and Respiratory System, pg. 27
>
> c. "Home groups" each have a number. The whole class now sends their "experts" #1, #2, #3, and #4's to sit together in designated areas of the class to read their paragraph. Each group of "experts" come to consensus on the content to be reported back to their "home group."
> d. The teacher signals the class to reassemble in their "home group" to report back. On command by the teacher, each expert now reports out to their home group the information they read.

2. Students learn to take pulse for aerobic activity lesson.

3. Jigsaw reading assignment on the FITT principles for cardiovascular fitness. (See FITT chart on page 102)

4. Homework: Find individual resting heart rate.

5. Students learn about stroke volume and how to calculate target heart rate zone.

6. Students write a description of the cardiovascular and respiratory system during exercise.

7. Each cooperative group gets one (1) piece of poster paper and one (1) packet of markers.

8. Students 1 and 2 draw the adult size of the heart and lungs on poster paper. Student 3 lies on the poster paper while student 4 traces around the body. They then draw the major veins and arteries of the body.

9. Display the oxygenated and non-oxygenated blood in the heart and lungs with the use of the blue and red markers. Have team members mark the arteries in red and the veins in blue. Direction arrows are used to show the flow of blood.

10. The heart and lungs are now pasted on the body and the veins and arteries are linked.

11. The team now completes the project with the following work:

    • description of the cardiovascular and respiratory system is taped on the poster

    • describe FIT principles on the poster

    • calculate THR zone on the poster

    • each team member selects one (1) aerobic activity they enjoy (list 4) and writes it on the poster

Program Results

This project included Howard Gardner's *Multiple Intelligences*.

- Verbal/Linguistic

- Logical/Mathematical

- Visual/Spacial

- Body/Kinesthetic

- Musical/Rhythmic

- Interpersonal

- Intrapersonal

If each student is capable of seven different methods of processing information and each person differs in the specific profile of intelligence they demonstrate, then education must incorporate into its system ways to better educate and meet the needs of all students. The students loved the project. Each person was able to contribute to the team's success through their method of learning.

Program Tips

Allow space to store the posters each day. Have students roll the posters up at the end of each class, put their name and period in the corner of the rolled poster and secure with a rubber band. This makes it easier to identify and distribute the posters each day. Use a cookie tin for the markers, glue sticks, and scissors. Students will get what they need and return all supplies at the end of the period.

Display posters for students and faculty to view as well as at an open house.

FITT PRINCIPAL: Threshold of Training and Fitness Target Zones

F	–	Frequency	How often
I	–	Intensity	How hard
T	–	Time	How long
T	–	Type	What kind

FIT principal is applied to the five components of fitness:

Cardiovascular Endurance	F=3x wk/more	I=Target Heart Rate Zone	T=30 mins
Muscle Strength	F=3x wk	I=60%-90% of max	T=Sets and Reps
Muscle Endurance	F=3x wk	I=own body weight	T=60 sec
Flexibility	F=3x wk/more	I=point of strain	T=30-60 sec
Body Composition			

CARDIOVASCULAR AND RESPIRATORY SYSTEMS DURING EXERCISE

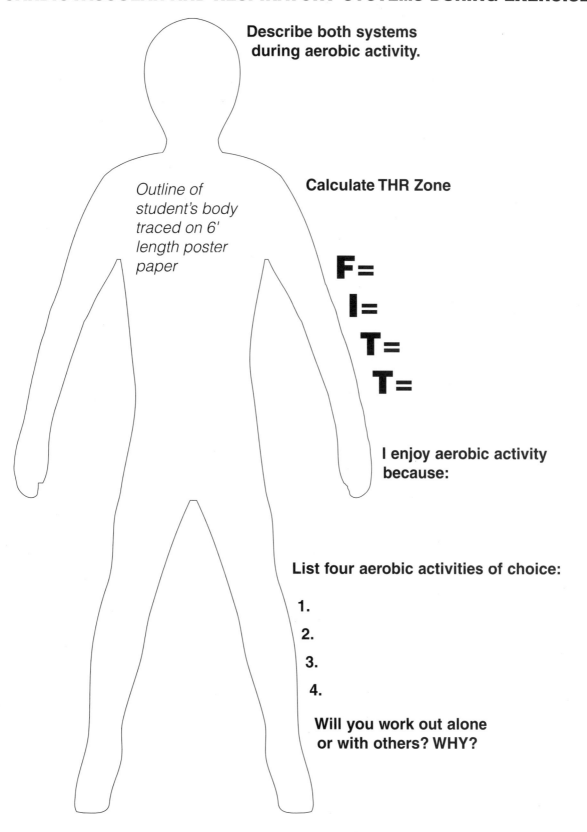

Describe both systems during aerobic activity.

Outline of student's body traced on 6' length poster paper

Calculate THR Zone

F=

I=

T=

T=

I enjoy aerobic activity because:

List four aerobic activities of choice:

1.

2.

3.

4.

Will you work out alone or with others? WHY?

Cardiovascular and Respiratory Systems During Exercise

Name _____ # _____ Name _____ # _____

Name _____ # _____ Name _____ # _____

Project Title: _____

CATEGORIES	POSSIBLE POINTS	EARNED POINTS	COMMENTS
Description	10		
FITT Principals	5		
Target Heart Rate	5		
Aerobic Activities	5		
Heart	5		
Lungs	5		
Circulation	5		
Body Chart	5		
TOTAL POINTS	**45**		

GRADING SCALE

45-40 A

39-35 B

34-30 C

29-25 D

24-20 F

Exercise Challenge

School: Baton Rouge High School
2825 Government Street
Baton Rouge, LA 70806
Phone: (504) 383-0520
Contributor: Almenia Freemen Williams, Physical Education
Disney Channel Teacher of the Year

Program Objectives

• to encourage extra physical activity for children

• to promote regular physical activity

• to encourage parental participation

Materials/Equipment Needed

• depends on the activity/activities chosen from the list

Procedures and Teaching Strategies

• use goals and rewards to encourage regular physical activity over a 12 week period

• encourage participation of High School students and their families

• urge students to exercise in groups as added motivation

Program Description

This activity involves the use of an EXERCISE LOG to track regular physical activity over a 12 week period. The project is initiated in the classroom but carried out after school and on weekends. Physical Education class time and team practices/ events do not count towards the goal.

Each week has 42 boxes and each box represents five (5) minutes of exercise. For each five (5) minutes of exercise, shade in one (1) box. Acceptable exercise activities are listed on the following page. At the end of the 12 week program, all boxes should be filled in. The completed log can then be exchanged for an EXERCISE CHALLENGE T-shirt.

ACCEPTABLE ACTIVITIES

Children (up to age 8)	**Youth, Teens, Adults** (Ages 9 - 55)	**Seniors*** (55 & over)
soccer	aerobic dancing	gardening
tennis	hiking	painting (walls)
walking	walking/jogging	changing a tire
jogging	running	raking leaves
bike riding	circuit weight training	sweeping driveway
jump rope	skiing (water/snow)	stairclimbing
swimming	golf	washing car/boat
basketball	handball	table tennis
rollerskating	racquetball	shuffleboard
	rollerskating	All Senior Olympic activities
	rowing	
	soccer	
	basketball	* In addition to all activities listed for other groups
	tennis	
	softball	
	stairclimbing (machine)	
	treadmill	
	swimming	

Program Tips

Awards such as T-shirts and printed certificates may be funded by a donation from a local company or a mini-grant available through your state associations, ie. AAHPERD.

Program graphic to be used on T-shirts and promotional materials could be determined through an art contest.

Plan an awards ceremony to distribute the T-shirts earned during the EXERCISE CHALLENGE. Make note of individual accomplishments made during this twelve week session. Challenge participants to continue "the exercise habit" with new and bigger goals.

Promote the accomplishments of the participants in the school newsletter, local newspapers and TV.

Tip: When reproducing for classroom handouts, copy pages 107 and 108 back to back.

Dear EXERCISE CHALLENGE Participant:

"A survey has shown that 90% of all Americans believe that participation in some kind of regular physical activity is important. Many are now realizing the value of being active and feeling fit no mater what their age. However, many people, both young and old, are not as physically fit as they should be. Studies have shown that too few children and teenagers can pass a simple test of physical fitness. More than 50% of all teenagers cannot do one chin-up, and only 55% of adult Americans do any kind of regular exercise.

Many people do only the least amount of exercise possible. Studies have shown that fitness declines with age. This lack of fitness is the result of our inactive life style that depends on the car, television, and other machines. You probably do not need a high level of fitness to live in a world that uses many machines, but regular physical activity is necessary if your body is to function properly. That is why it is important to follow a regular exercise program."

Fitness For Life
Carbin and Lindsey

ACCEPTABLE ACTIVITIES

Children	**Youth, Teens, Adults**	**Seniors***
(up to age 8)	(Ages 9 - 55)	(55 & over)
soccer	aerobic dancing	gardening
tennis	hiking	painting (walls)
walking	walking/jogging	changing a tire
jogging	running	raking leaves
bike riding	circuit weight training	sweeping driveway
jump rope	skiing (water/snow)	stairclimbing
swimming	golf	washing car/boat
basketball	handball	table tennis
rollerskating	racquetball	shuffleboard
	rollerskating	All Senior Olympic activities
	rowing	
	soccer	
	basketball	* In addition to all activities
	tennis	listed for other groups
	softball	
	stairclimbing (machine)	
	treadmill	
	swimming	

NAME _____

ADDRESS _____

TELEPHONE _____

T-shirt size (circle one)   **XXL**   **XL**   **L**   **M**   **S**   **14-16**   **10-12**
($1.00 extra)

SAMPLE

TIP: When reproducing for classroom handouts, copy pages 107 and 108 back to back.

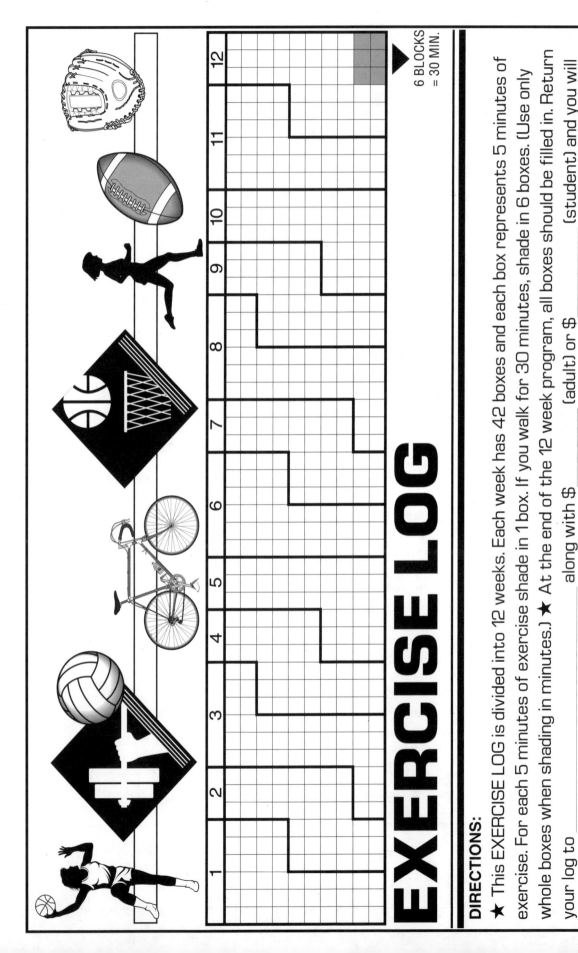

EXERCISE LOG

6 BLOCKS = 30 MIN.

DIRECTIONS:

★ This EXERCISE LOG is divided into 12 weeks. Each week has 42 boxes and each box represents 5 minutes of exercise. For each 5 minutes of exercise shade in 1 box. If you walk for 30 minutes, shade in 6 boxes. (Use only whole boxes when shading in minutes.) ★ At the end of the 12 week program, all boxes should be filled in. Return your log to _____ along with $_____ (adult) or $_____ (student) and you will receive a T-shirt with the EXERCISE CHALLENGE logo on it. You may choose to do this every 12 weeks, however T-shirts are given only once. ★ Physical Education class time and team practices do not count.

PROGRAM:

Holistic and Preventive Medicine

School:
Health Careers Academy
Bell Gardens High School
6119 Agra Street
Bell Gardens, CA 90201

Phone: (213) 773-3871

Contributor: Carolyn Thompson–NASPE NATIONAL TEACHER OF THE YEAR

Program Objectives

• to design a life long fitness plan

• to understand why healthy choices, activity and fitness determine how long one may live

• to identify risk factors

Materials/Equipment Needed

• large sheets of colored construction paper

• 4'-5' lengths of poster paper

• a collection of fitness magazines for pictures (ask students and teachers to bring)

• video tape and camera

• Textbooks:
Fitness For Life, by Charles B. Corbin and Ruth Lindsey (Glenview, IL: Scott, Foresman and Company 1979).

Personal Fitness: Looking Good/Feeling Good, by Charles S. Williams, Emmanouel G. Harageones, DeWayne J. Johnson, and Charles D. Smith (Dubuque, IA: Kendall/Hunt Publishing Company 1986).

Moving For Life, by Gary B. Spindt, William H. Monti and Betty Hennessy, Ph.D. (Dubuque, IA: Kendall/Hunt Publishing Company 1991).

Basic Stuff Series I, by Pat Dodds, Editor (Reston, VA: American Alliance for Health, Physical Education, Recreation and Dance 1987).

Procedures and Teaching Strategies

• use knowledge gained from research to develop a lifetime plan of activity

Program Description

PERSONAL FITNESS PLAN

A series of personal assessments are experienced each day for six weeks. Such assessments may include a risk factor sheet, Max VO2 sheet, target heart rate chart, vital capacity, stress test, blood pressure, physical fitness test, growth and development chart, calorie intake and calorie output, and metabolic rate. The students identify good health habits and poor health habits according to the data collected. With this research and information, the students design their own personal fitness plan by using the principles and components of fitness. The students learn how to change their behavior to avoid risk and stay healthy. The assignment is collected in notebook form at the end of the unit.

Questions are written in the borders of the students' notebooks as they are being graded. The life plan is returned to the student for further input. This exchange is continued until it is evident that the student has grasped the concept being questioned.

LONGEVITY FITNESS PLAN

The longevity assessment is given after the personal fitness plan is completed. The students will determine an anticipated life span. With this information, the students will identify what they plan to be doing at certain points in time in their lives. The students must select the kind of activity they will use to stay active in their 20's, their 30's, their 40's, their 50's, their 60's, their 70's, their 80's, and their 90's. This assignment may be a two to three week task depending upon the amount of time given to the students in class to work on this project. This aspect of their assignment really brings the students into focus with their lives, their goals, and their education.

The product may take one of the following forms in its design:

- video tape
- diary format
- mural
- time line
- mobile

Encourage students to outline and prepare how they will introduce their longevity fitness plan. Have all of the materials available for the students to begin once the preparation phase is completed. Students then display their project and share their lifetime fitness plan with others.

Program Results

Personal assessment involving physiology of exercise is a great motivator for students to understand the why's of exercise. They enjoyed learning about their body and their attitude toward fitness. The personal fitness plan can be revisited any time in their life once the concepts are understood.

The longevity assignment thrilled the students. To determine their own future and its destiny gave a great deal of meaning to who they will become. The products will excite you as a teacher.

Program Tips

Allow students the opportunity to process information in a learning style relevant for them.

Encourage students to come up with additional formats for the project. Challenge their creativity.

Have students display completed projects during an open house.

LIFE CHOICE INVENTORY: HOW LONG WILL YOU LIVE?

How long will you live? No one can answer this question for sure, of course. But you can increase or decrease your probable life expectancy by a good many years depending on what choices you make. That is, your statistical chances of dying younger or older are affected by how you live.

The Longevity Game illustrates this principle. To play the game, start on the top line (age 74, the average life expectancy for adults in the United States today). Then answer the 11 questions that follow. For each question, add or subtract years as instructed. If a question doesn't apply, go on to the next one. If you are not sure of the exact number to add or subtract, make a guess. Don't take the score too seriously, but do pay attention to those areas where you lose years: they could point to choices you might want to change.

Start with:	74	7. Smoking	____
1. Exercise	____	8. Drinking	____
2. Relaxation	____	9. Gender	____
3. Driving	____	10. Weight	____
4. Blood pressure	____	11. Age	____
5. 65 and working	____		
6. Family history	____	**Your final score**	____

1. Exercise. If your work requires regular, vigorous activity or you work out each day, add three years. If you don't get much exercise at home, work, or play, subtract three years.

2. Relaxation. If you have a relaxed approach to life (you roll with the punches), add three years. If you're aggressive, ambitious, or nervous (you have sleepless nights, you bite your nails), subtract three years. If you consider yourself unhappy, subtract another year.

3. Driving. Drivers under 30 who have had a traffic ticket in the last year or have been involved in an accident, subtract four years. Other violations, minus one. If you always wear seat belts, add one.

4. Blood pressure. High blood pressure is a major cause of the most common killers – heart attacks and strokes – but most victims don't know they have it. If you know you have it, you are likely to do something about it. If you know your blood pressure, add one year.

5. Sixty-five and working. If you are 65 or older and still working, add three.

6. Family history. If any grandparent reached age 85, add two. If all grandparents have reached age 80, add six. If a parent died of a stroke or heart attack before age 50, minus four. If a parent or brother or sister has (or had) diabetes since childhood, minus three years.

7. Smoking. Cigarette smokers who finish: More than two packs a day, minus eight years. One or two packs a day, minus six years. One-half to one pack a day, minus three years.

8. Drinking. If you drink two cocktails (or beers or glasses of wine) a day, subtract one year. For each additional daily libation, subtract two.

9. Gender. Women live longer than men. Females add three years, males subtract three years.

10. Weight. If you avoid eating fatty foods and don't add salt to your meals, your heart will be healthier, and you're entitled to add two years. Now, weigh in: Overweight by 50 pounds or more, minus eight years. 30-40 pounds, minus four years. 10-29 pounds, minus two.

11. Age. How long you have already lived can help predict how much longer you'll live. If you're under 30, the jury is still out. But if your age is 30-39, plus two. 40-49, plus three. 50-69, plus four. 70 or over, plus five.

Tip: When reproducing for classroom handouts, copy pages 112 and 113 back to back.

HOW I FEEL ABOUT EXERCISE PROGRAMS

This self-evaluation is meant to help you understand your reasons for participating in exercise and sports. It contains statements that will tell you more about yourself. There is no right or wrong answer.

DOING THE SELF-EVALUATION. This self-evaluation contains sets of three statements each. Read each statement. Check only the box before the statement or statements that honestly tell how you feel. In some sets you may have no checks. Then read the instructions on the following pages to score this self evaluation.

Set		Statement
1.	☐	I prefer to do activities with others.
	☐	It is difficult for me to be motivated to exercise alone.
	☐	My principal reason for doing activities and exercise is to meet and be with people.
2.	☐	I prefer activities in which I can laugh.
	☐	I do not prefer activities or exercises that are monotonous.
	☐	I find fun in most exercises and activities.
3.	☐	I prefer exercises that tax my ability.
	☐	I prefer activities that force me to work hard.
	☐	I do not like activities or exercises that are too easy.
4.	☐	I prefer competitive activities.
	☐	I like to compare my ability to that of others.
	☐	I do not like to lose.
5.	☐	I am most interested in attaining physical fitness.
	☐	I prefer to do exercises and activities where I must move a lot.
	☐	My principal reason for exercising and participating is for attaining better health.
6.	☐	I desire to exercise mainly to improve my figure or build.
	☐	I want to exercise to improve the way I look.
	☐	I do not care for activities that will not make me look more youthful.
7.	☐	I like activities that help me relax.
	☐	I don't like activities that are complicated and make me nervous.
	☐	I feel better doing activities in which I can feel at ease.
8.	☐	I like to do activities that I don't already know.
	☐	I like to do new exercises and games.
	☐	I don't like to follow a routine that I am familiar with when exercising.
9.	☐	I like to do exercises and games with people my own age.
	☐	I don't like younger more capable people to watch me exercise and participate in sports.
	☐	I like to do activities with people less capable or equal to my ability.
10.	☐	I prefer to know why I am doing an exercise.
	☐	I like to know what part of my body is benefited by the activity.
	☐	I don't like to be told to do something for which I don't understand the value.

Tip: When reproducing for classroom handouts, copy pages 112 and 113 back to back.

HOW I FEEL ABOUT EXERCISE PROGRAMS
SCORE SHEET

SCORING THE SELF-EVALUATION. You have read and checked the statements that describe how you feel. Now do the following: Add up the number of checks in each separate set. Record the number in each set by checking the appropriate boxes in the rating section below. Read the score description for each set to see what your rating in that area means. There is no best way to feel about exercise and sports. You may want to think about why you have a low score in some areas and a medium or high score in others. This will give you some idea of your feelings toward regular physical activity.

Set	Rating Low (0 or 1 check)	Medium (2 checks)	High (3 checks)	Score Name and Description
1.	☐	☐	☐	**Social Score** People who have a high Social Score like exercise and sports because they like to be with other people.
2.	☐	☐	☐	**Enjoyment Score** People who have a high Enjoyment Score feel that a major reason for exercising is for the fun of it.
3.	☐	☐	☐	**Training Score** People who have a high Training Score like exercise because they like to see what they can do physically.
4.	☐	☐	☐	**Competition Score** People who have a high Competition Score like to see how they compare with other people.
5.	☐	☐	☐	**Health Score** People who have a high Health Score believe that they should exercise for their health and fitness and because it makes them feel good.
6.	☐	☐	☐	**Appearance Score** People who have a high Appearance Score like to exercise because they believe it will make them look better.
7.	☐	☐	☐	**Relaxation Score** People who have a high Relaxation Score believe that exercise is good for reducing stress and for relaxing after a stressful day.
8.	☐	☐	☐	**New Experience Score** People who have a high New Experience Score like to be challenged to learn new things.
9.	☐	☐	☐	**Peer Score** People who have a high Peer Score like to participate with their own age group.
10.	☐	☐	☐	**Desire Knowledge Score** People who have a high Desire Knowledge Score like to understand and gain knowledge.

Tip: When reproducing for classroom handouts, copy pages 114 and 115 back to back.

STUDENT CARD

WELLNESS ASSESSMENT

These statements are designed to help you assess your health and add to your awareness and understanding of your overall health. Circle the number before each statement which you believe to be an accurate description of yourself.

SECTION 1 Nutrition

1. I limit my consumption of high-fat foods (eggs, dairy products, fatty meats, fried foods).
2. I limit my consumption of salt and salty foods.
3. I eat fish and poultry more often than I eat red meat.
4. I eat 5 servings of fruits and vegetables a day.
5. I limit my intake of sweets, sodas, and snack foods.
6. I drink several glasses of water a day.

SECTION 2 Emotional Well-Being

1. I laugh often and easily.
2. I can ask for help when needed.
3. I include relaxation time as part of my daily schedule.
4. I have someone with whom I can discuss personal problems.
5. I can express concern and love to those I care about.
6. I can express my angry feelings rather than hold them in.
7. There is a healthy balance between my work (school and job) and leisure time.

SECTION 3 Fitness

1. I am within the normal weight range for my gender, height and age.
2. I keep in shape by doing vigorous exercise (biking, swimming, running, sports, aerobics, etc.) for at least 30 minutes three times a week or doing moderate exercise (like walking) an hour a day.
3. I stretch, do yoga, or move my body regularly in a variety of ways to keep it supple and flexible.
4. I regularly engage in activities (weight training, work that involves heavy objects, sports that work the whole body) that develop over-all strength.
5. I am pleased with the way I look and feel.
6. I have enough energy to do the things I like to do.

SECTION 4 Family History

I have a family member who:
1. Had a heart attack.
2. Had or has high blood pressure.
3. Developed diabetes as an adult.
4. Had or has breast cancer.
5. Had or has a drug or alcohol problem.

SECTION 5 Alcohol, Nicotine, and Other Drug Use

1. I do not smoke cigarettes or chew tobacco.
2. I do not use alcohol.
3. I do not use marijuana or other drugs.
4. I ask about the side effects of any prescribed medications.
5. I read and follow the instructions on all prescribed or over-the-counter medications.
6. I ask about the effect of taking more than one medication at a time.
7. I am aware of the dangers of alcohol, nicotine, and other drugs.

SECTION 6 Accidents

1. I do not accept rides from drivers who have been drinking or taking drugs.
2. I wear a seat belt whenever I am in an automobile.
3. I wear a helmet when I ride a bicycle or motorcycle.
4. I obey all traffic and safety rules.

SECTION 7 Human Values

1. I take part in activities that stimulate me intellectually.
2. I participate in family, church and/or community activities.
3. I stand by my own values even when they are different from those of my friends.
4. I use my thoughts and attitudes in life-affirming ways.
5. I accept other people's ideas and values even though they may be different from my own.
6. I believe in a positive force that supports my well-being.

SECTION 8 Self-Care

1. I have yearly dental and medical check-ups.
2. I get at least 8 hours of sleep a day or sufficient sleep for me to awaken feeling rested.
3. I am aware of bodily changes that might indicate a health problem.
4. I know how to do self-examinations.
5. When I am ill, I rest and follow the doctor's treatment.
6. I know what to do in case of illness or injury.
7. I do not participate in behavior that could be dangerous to my health.
8. I know how to prevent the transmission of STD, and HIV/AIDS.

HEALING and the **MIND** with Bill Moyers

SECTION	1	2	3	4	5	6	7
				(omit)			

Write the number of statements you circled for each section.

Tip: When reproducing for classroom handouts, copy pages 114 and 115 back to back.

STUDENT CARD
WELLNESS ASSESSMENT

A PORTRAIT OF YOUR HEALTH

Use your responses for each section to complete the graph. The results will give you an overall picture of how you view your health. For each section, shade one box for each statement you circled.

EXAMPLE:

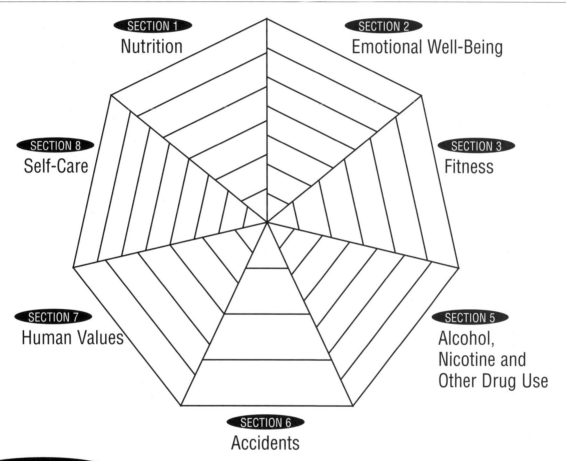

SECTION 1
Nutrition

SECTION 2
Emotional Well-Being

SECTION 8
Self-Care

SECTION 3
Fitness

SECTION 7
Human Values

SECTION 5
Alcohol, Nicotine and Other Drug Use

SECTION 6
Accidents

EVALUATION KEY

Completely Shaded Sections:
Healthy behavior and life-style choices. Keep it up!

Partially Shaded Sections:
A little more effort and attention to these issues can improve the quality and length of your life. Work a little harder!

Barely or Not At All Shaded Sections:
There is significant room for improving your health in these areas. First, work on areas where you feel confident of success, then attack the areas that are more difficult for you.

NOTE: This graph does not include Section 4: Family History, since you have no control over this area of your life. However, it is helpful to be aware of health issues that may be hereditary and use this awareness to pay particular attention to preventative steps that can help you avoid these conditions.

This self-assessment card was prepared by Thirteen/WNET based on a concept developed by the editors of the Wellness Letter at the University of California at Berkeley.

HOW DOES YOUR STRESS SCORE?

Name _____ Date _____ Class _____

Purpose: The following scale will help you determine how much stress changes in your life may be causing.

Procedures: Some stress is necessary for life, but too much stress is harmful. A scale has been developed for measuring stress in terms of life's daily events. The chart below is adapted to a teenager's life. To find your score, check the events applying to you during the past 12 months, and look at the point value assigned to that event. Then add up your points. A score of 300+ means you have an 80 percent chance of becoming seriously ill.

	Point Value	Event
_____	100	1. Death of parent or other significant adult
_____	73	2. Divorce of parents
_____	65	3. Marital separation of parents
_____	63	4. Jail term for you
_____	53	5. Personal injury or illness
_____	50	6. Marriage
_____	47	7. Fired from your full time work
_____	45	8. Marital reconciliation of parents
_____	45	9. Remarriage of parents
_____	44	10. Change in family member's health
_____	40	11. Pregnancy
_____	39	12. Low grades received
_____	39	13. Addition to your family
_____	39	14. Breaking up of a relationship
_____	38	15. A change in your financial status
_____	37	16. Death of a close friend
_____	36	17. Getting a part time job
_____	35	18. Change in the number of family arguments
_____	31	19. Fired from a part time job
_____	30	20. Changing jobs
_____	29	21. A change in work or school responsibilities
_____	29	22. Brother or sister leaving home
_____	29	23. Trouble with parents or siblings
_____	29	24. Outstanding personal achievement
_____	26	25. Trouble with school
_____	26	26. Starting or finishing school
_____	26	27. A change in living conditions
_____	24	28. A change in personal habits
_____	23	29. Trouble with your boss
_____	20	30. Change in working hours, or conditions
_____	20	31. Change in residence
_____	20	32. Change in schools
_____	19	33. Change in your recreational habits
_____	19	34. Change in religious activities
_____	18	35. Change in social activities
_____	17	36. Disagreement with a friend
_____	16	37. Change in sleeping habits
_____	15	38. Change in number of family gatherings
_____	15	39. Change in eating habits
_____	13	40. Vacation
_____	12	41. The Christmas season
_____	11	42. Minor violation of the law

_____ **Total Points** *What does this mean to me?*

PERSONAL DATA

Name _____ Date _____

	Pre-test	**Post-Test**
Age	_____	_____
Resting Heart Rate	_____	_____

	Pre-test Date _____		**Post-test** Date _____	
	Score	Percentile	Score	Percentile
12 Minute Run	____	_____	____	_____
Skinfolds	____	_____	____	_____
_____ **#1**	____	_____	____	_____
_____ **#2**	____	_____	____	_____
_____ **#3**	____	_____	____	_____
Sit-ups	____	_____	____	_____
Sit-and-reach	____	_____	____	_____
Pull-ups	____	_____	____	_____

....

COMPUTING YOUR TARGET HEART ZONE

Purpose:　　　　To identify a target heart rate zone which is the safe and comfortable level of overload that should be maintained to achieve a training effect.

Procedures:	Example	Lower Limit	Upper Limit
1. Obtain your maximum heart rate according to your age. 220 - age = maximum heart rate	220 -14 206 MHR	220 -	220 -
2. Determine your resting heart rate and subtract from Step 1.	-70 RHR =136	_____	_____
3. What percent overload do you wish to train? The lower limit is 60% for training effect and the safe upper limit is 90%.	X.60%	X.60%	X.90%
4. Multiply Step 3 times the value of Step 2.	=81	=	=
5. Add the resting heart rate.	+70 RHR	+	+
6. A is the lower limit of heart rate for training effect and B is the safe upper limit.	**151**	**A=**	**B=**

Tip: When reproducing for classroom handouts, copy pages 118 and 119 back to back.

MAX VO₂ WORK SHEET

Name _____   Period _____

ESTIMATING CURRENT LEVEL OF CARDIOVASCULAR FITNESS

Directions: It is absolutely imperative that you give your best effort. Only then will you and your instructor be able to get an accurate assessment.

Run as far as you can in 12 minutes. You will achieve the best results if you start out and run at a comfortable and even pace for the first 9 to 10 minutes. During the last 2 minutes you should run faster, so that at the end of the test you are extremely tired. Every several yards makes a difference in the score, so do not quit until the teacher tells you.

Have your partner count the number of cones passed during the 12 minute run. Count the laps at first and then the cones as time enters the last two minutes. The cones are 20 yds. apart for a total of 22 cones per lap.

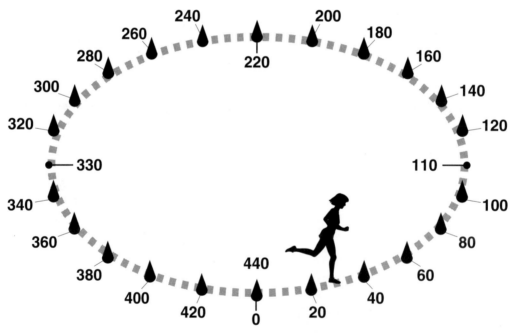

1 Lap = 22 cones x 20 yds. = 440 yds. per lap or distance covered.

440 yds
X _____ laps

A. [_____]

20 yds
X _____ cones

B. [_____]

A. [_____]

B. [_____]

[_____]

Tip: When reproducing for classroom handouts, copy pages 118 and 119 back to back.

ESTIMATING YOUR MAX. VO$_2$

Name	Date

Instructor	Period

Objective: Students will estimate their own max. VO$_2$ and compare it with a standardized chart to determine their level of cardiovascular endurance.

Directions: This is a very critical exam in being able to evaluate your current level of cardiovascular fitness. It is absolutely imperative that you give your best effort. Only then will you and your instructor be able to get an accurate assessment!

Run as far as you can in 12 minutes. You will achieve the best results if you start out and run at a comfortable and even pace for the first 9 to 10 minutes. During the last 2 minutes you should run faster, so that at the end of the test you are extremely tired. Every several yards makes a difference in the score, so do not quit until the teacher tells you.

1.

(distance covered in yards)

2.

(estimated VO$_2$ from charts)

3.

(percentile score from charts)

Questions: Based on your percentile rank, how do you feel about your current level of fitness? Are you above average or below average in your level of fitness? What do you plan to do about it?

Estimating oxygen consumption (VO$_2$) from 12 minute run.

Yards	*Estimated VO$_2$	Yards	*Estimated VO$_2$	Yards	*Estimated VO$_2$
3600	55.9	2850	45.5	2100	35.0
3550	55.2	2800	44.7	2050	34.2
3500	54.5	2750	44.0	2000	33.5
3450	53.9	2700	43.2	1950	32.8
3400	53.3	2650	42.9	1900	32.0
3350	52.6	2600	42.6	1850	31.2
3300	52.0	2550	42.0	1800	30.4
3250	51.3	2500	41.1	1750	29.6
3200	50.7	2450	40.3	1700	28.6
3150	50.0	2400	39.5	1650	27.4
3100	49.2	2350	38.8	1600	26.0
3050	48.5	2300	38.0	1550	24.4
3000	47.7	2250	37.3	1500	21.9
2950	47.0	2200	36.5	1450	19.3
2900	46.2	2150	35.8		

Range of maximal oxygen uptake value with age.*

MALES *Maximal Oxygen Uptake, ml/kg-min*

Age Group (Yr.)	Low	Fair	Average	Good	High
10-19	Below 38	38-46	47-56	57-66	above 66

FEMALES *Maximal Oxygen Uptake, ml/kg-min*

Age Group (Yr.)	Low	Fair	Average	Good	High
10-19	Below 30	30-38	38-46	47-56	above 56

DETERMINING YOUR BLOOD PRESSURE

Objective: Students will determine their blood pressure.

Directions: Using the equipment supplied by your instructor, you are to take the blood pressure of a classmate. Do the test at least three times, or until you can obtain three readings that are nearly the same.

The test is given with a sphygmomanometer, which is a rubber cuff that is wrapped around the arm as shown by your teacher. The cuff is inflated with air until it momentarily closes off the artery in the arm. Using the valve, slowly release air until you hear the first "thump." This is the systolic pressure. The second sound you will hear as you continually release the valve is a "swish" sound. This is the diastolic pressure. Record the values.

	①	②	③
Systolic Pressure	_____	_____	_____
Diastolic Pressure	_____	_____	_____

Tip: When reproducing for classroom handouts, copy pages 121 and 122 back to back.

CALORIC COST OF ACTIVITIES

Name   Class   Date

Purpose: This activity will help you determine the number of calories you use while participating in various activities.

Procedure: 1. Keep track of how much time you spend on each activity.

2. Record the date, the name of the activity, the calories per minute per pound, your weight, and the number of minutes you participated in the activity on the form provided.

3. Determine the number of calories you used for each activity by multiplying the calories per minute per pound *times* your weight *times* the number of minutes you performed the activity.

_____ X _____ X _____ = _____
cal./min./lb.   weight   minutes   calories

Date	Activity	Cal./Min./Lb.	Weight	Minutes	Calories

EXAMPLE

Date	Activity	Cal./Min./Lb.	Weight	Minutes	Calories
	Hiking	.042	150	60	378

Tip: When reproducing for classroom handouts, copy pages 121 and 122 back to back.

TABLE 1 · CALORIC COST OF SELECTED ACTIVITIES

Activity	Cal./Min.	Cal./Hour/Lb. for 150 Pound Person	Activity	Cal./Min.	Cal./Hour/Lb. for 150 Pound Person
Archery	.034	305	**Judo**	.087	785
Badminton:			**Karate**	.087	785
moderate	.039	350	**Mountain Climbing**	.086	775
vigorous	.065	585	**Paddleball**	.069	620
Baseball:			**Rowing:**		
infield-outfield	.031	280	moderate (2.5 mph)	.036	325
pitching	.039	350	vigorous	.118	1060
Basketball:			**Running:**		
moderate	.047	420	6 mph (10 min./mile)	.079	710
vigorous	.066	595	10 mph (6 min./mile	.1	900
Bicycling:			12 mph (5 min./mile)	.13	1170
slow (5 mph)	.025	225	**Sailing**	.02	180
moderate (10 mph)	.05	450	**Skating:**		
fast (13 mph)	.072	650	moderate	.036	325
Bowling	.028	255	vigorous	.064	575
Calisthenics	.045	405	**Skiing** (snow):		
Canoeing:			downhill	.059	530
2.5 mph	.023	210	level (5 mph)	.078	700
4.0 mph	.047	420	**Soccer**	.063	570
Dancing:			**Squash**	.07	630
slow	.029	260	**Stationary Running:**		
moderate	.045	405	70-80 counts/min.	.078	700
fast	.064	575	**Swimming** (crawl):		
Fencing:			20 yards/min.	.032	290
moderate	.033	300	45 yards/min.	.058	520
vigorous	.057	515	50 yards/min.	.071	640
Fishing	.016	145	**Table Tennis:**		
Football (tag)	.04	360	moderate	.026	235
Golf	.029	260	vigorous	.04	360
Gymnastics:			**Tennis:**		
light	.022	200	moderate	.046	415
heavy	.056	505	vigorous	.06	540
Handball	.063	570	**Volleyball:**		
Hiking	.042	375	moderate	.036	325
Hill Climbing	.06	540	vigorous	.065	585
Horseback Riding:			**Walking**	.033	300
walk	.019	175	**Water Skiing**	.053	480
trot	.046	415	**Wrestling**	.091	820
gallop	.067	600			
Jogging:					
4.5 mph (13:30 mile)	.063	565			

WALKHARD WORKOUT CHART

NAME _____ # _____ PERIOD _____

WEEK	TIME (MIN)	FREQUENCY (X/WEEK)	% TARGET HEART RATE	SPEED/mph (APPROX)	DISTANCE (APPROX ML)	CALORIC BURN
1 - 2	20	3	50 - 60%	2.0 - 2.5	0.5 - 1.0	60 - 80
3 - 4	30	3	60 - 65%	2.5 - 3.0	1.0 - 1.5	100 - 125
5 - 6	40	4	65 - 70%	3.0 - 3.5	1.5 - 2.0	150 - 200
7 - 8	45	4	65 - 70%	3.0 - 3.5	2.0 - 2.5	250 - 275
9 - 10	50	5	70 - 75%	3.5 - 4.0	3.0 - 3.5	275 - 300
11 - 12	60	5	75 - 80%	3.5 - 4.0	3.5 - 4.0	300 - 350

From Reebok International Corporation

GRAPHING

Fitness and math can be combined by graphing the running results.

One of the aims of recording is to give feedback on individual improvement.

Bar or line graphs recorded in the physical activity diaries or on charts will highlight this improvement.

This can be done in the following ways:

IMPROVEMENT GRAPHS

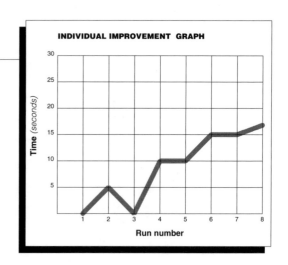

Individually

Class members calculate their improvement and graph it (fast and slow runners will have similar graphs).

As a class

Calculate the overall class improvement (there may be some minus values) and graph it. The person with the greatest improvement could be responsible for recording the graph for that day.

ABSOLUTE VALUE GRAPH

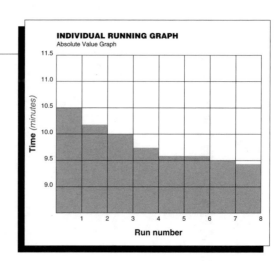

The actual time/distance run by each student or the whole class can be graphed.

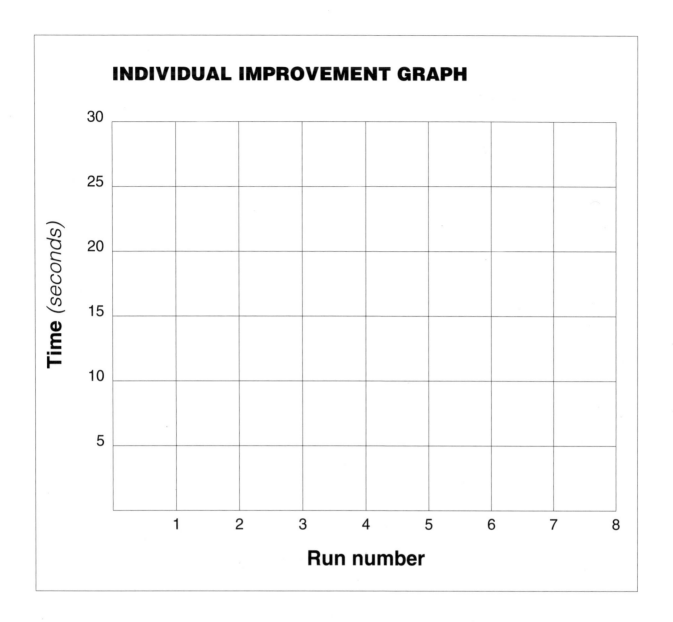

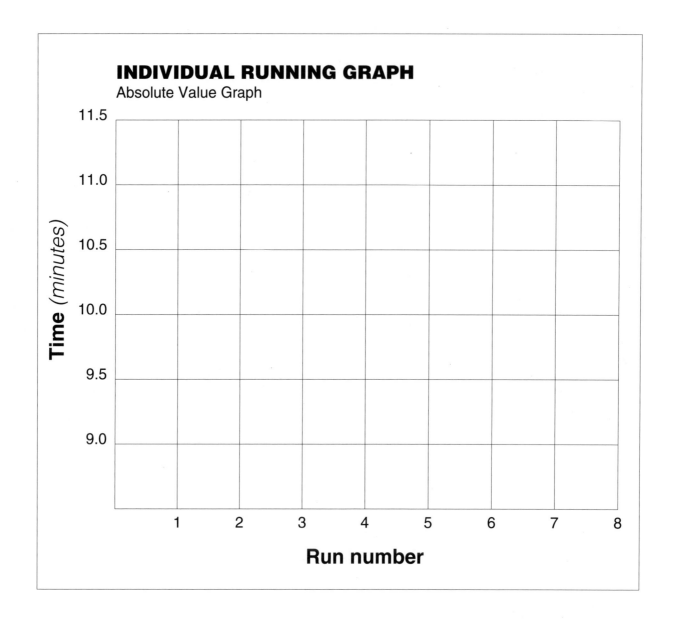

RUN AROUND AUSTRALIA

Decide on a town or city to which your class would like to run. It may be a place you will be studying in social studies, or near an area you will be visiting later in the year; or it could be a school somewhere in the state with which you will be conducting an inter-school exchange. A more ambitious idea would be for the whole school to try to run around Australia. The route may be as short or as long as you like.

Then measure the route which will be used for the runs.

To score, add up the distance the class runs in each session and plot that distance on a large map hanging in the classroom. If there are 30 children in the class, and each one runs 1km, then the class has travelled 30kms from the school toward the destination.

Draw a large map or diagram of the route to be taken and after each run mark down the progress made toward the destination.

As an option, plan the route so that it passes through areas to be studied later. On "reaching" each area, visit it, have the lessons on it, or do some activities related to it.

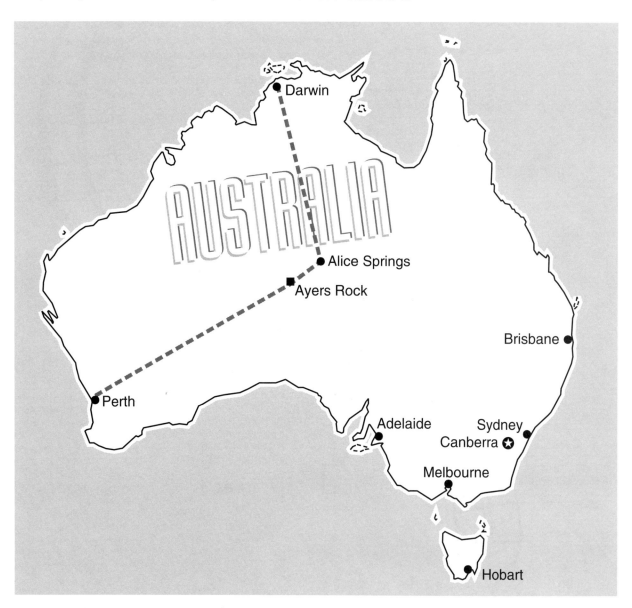

RUN TO

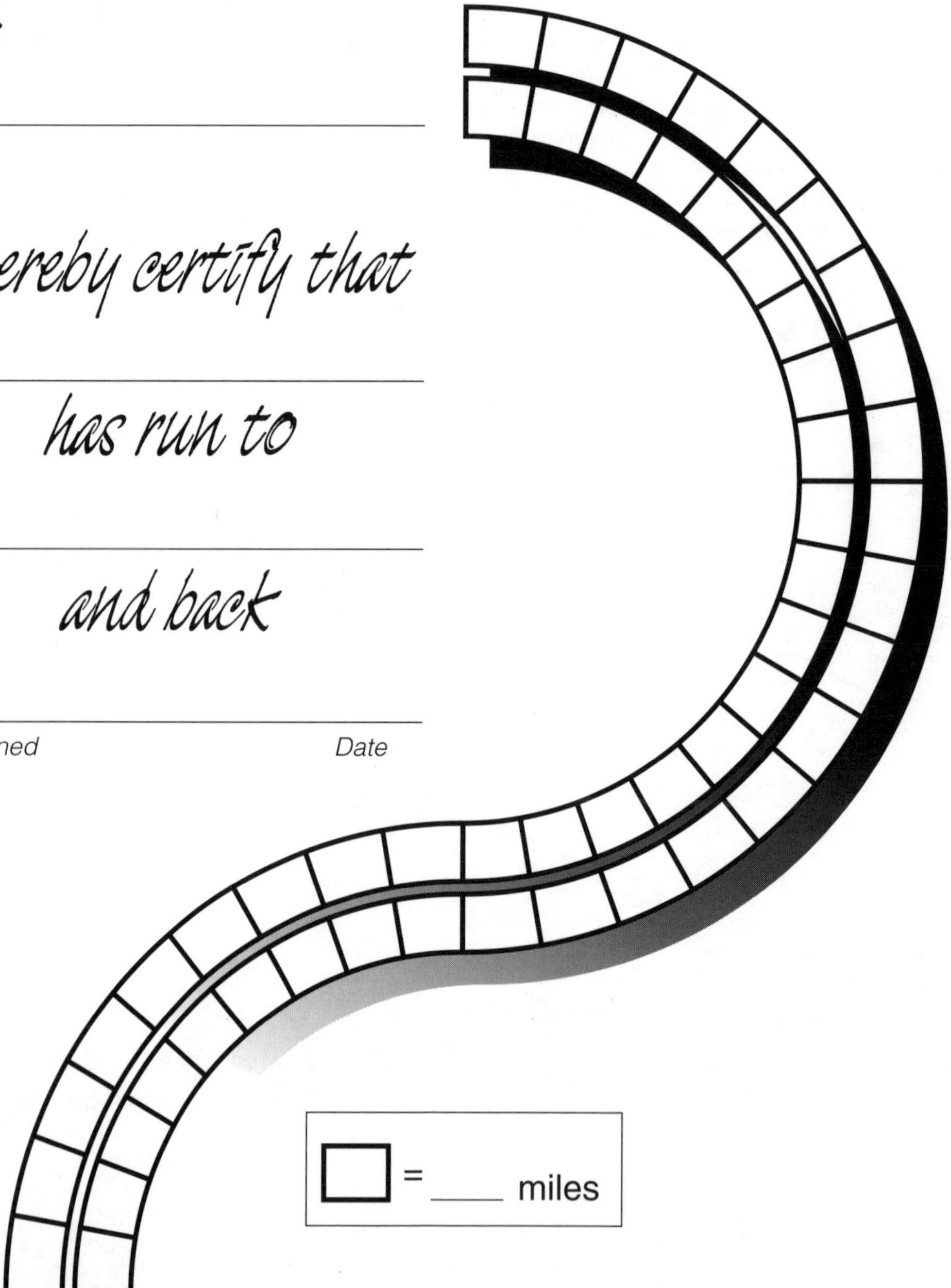

_____

I hereby certify that

_____

has run to

_____

and back

_____
Signed   Date

□ = _____ miles

Human Performance

School: Wasilla Middle School
650 Bogard Road
Wasilla, AK 99654
Phone: (907) 376-5308
Contributor: Rosalie Schuette–NASPE DISTRICT TEACHER OF THE YEAR

Program Objectives

• to design and apply a human performance program based on researched training techniques

• to design and apply a nutrition program based on researched information

• to keep a log to document improvements

• to upgrade fitness level of students

• to teach students assessment and evaluation techniques

Materials/Equipment Needed

• Human Performance Lab – exercise bicycles, rowing machines, treadmills, bicycle ergometer, skinfold calipers, blood pressure kits, lung capacity assessment devices, skeleton, and anatomy and physiology charts

• Weight Room – free weight stations for bench and squat, dumbbells, curling bars, isolation machines such as the Roman chair

• Auxiliary Weight Room – multi-station weight machines such as Universal, upper body and lower body stations

Procedures and Teaching Strategies

• allow students to design and create a personalized program that meets their needs

• keep a log of their day-to-day progress in a journal (notebook or portfolio) to document improvements in their human performance program

• assess and evaluate each other as they complete research and lab activities for their human performance profile

Program Description

This program allows students to design and create a personalized program that meets their needs. The physical education teacher works with each student at the beginning of the class to help them identify their goals. Goals may be to attain a higher level of fitness, to enhance their sport performance, or to help them achieve a personal goal such as competing in a body building contest. The physical education teacher consults with the student throughout the course to help them achieve their specific goal or to help them modify their program.

The program was created to involve students in the 11th and 12th grades. Students may take the human performance course once during their junior year and once during their senior year since the human performance program is individualized and new and varied topics are discussed. The class is limited to 20 students.

A. Identification of Goals

Each student spends time with the physical education instructor to clarify their goal/s for the semester. The more specific the goal, as well as the steps needed to obtain the goal, the better the chances of it happening.

B. Working Out

Students work out four (4) days per week. The other day is set aside for lecture/lab activities, topic discussions and research. Student profile assessments and computer lab assignments are also done on this day.

C. Record Keeping

Students keep weekly logs depicting their progress. A human performance profile is kept which includes pre/post assessment data.

D. Evaluation

The progress of the student is assessed by reviewing their weekly logs, and by reviewing their human performance profile which includes pre/post assessment data. The students must also complete a written exam where they are asked to utilize the knowledge and application from the course and apply this to a number of cases by analyzing, assessing, and prescribing a human performance program.

E. Other Supplemental Material

- step-up boxes

- jump ropes

- video instruction tapes of aerobic workouts

- computer program for performance assessment such as the one used in conjunction with Hoeger's Principles and Labs for Physical Fitness and Wellness lab text book

Program Results

This program helped students take responsibility for their own personalized fitness and exercise program while in school.

Note: The human performance lab is utilized as a wellness center for certified and classified employees in the building before school, during lunch, and after school.

Program Tips

Involve students from this class in the orientation of new users to the school's human performance lab. Students could conduct fitness assessments, develop exercise prescriptions and provide guidance in goal setting for students from a freshman fitness class or weight training class.

Invite the local media to hear about your program.

Hold an open house for parents of the students in the Human Performance class. Invite them to visit the lab and have the students available to conduct basic assessments.

Enlist the support of top school administrators for your program. Their backing is vital to the success of the program. Be sure to show them the many ways this program can generate positive publicity about your school.

Personal Fitness

School: Appleton West High School
610 N. Badger Avenue
Appleton, WI 54914
Phone: (414) 832-6219
Contributor: John Kading–Physical Education Chair
NASPE TEACHER OF THE YEAR

Program Objectives

• to gain an understanding of health related physical fitness

• to get students involved in designing a personal fitness program specifically targeted to their own individual fitness preferences and levels

Materials/Equipment Needed

• <u>Personal Fitness: Looking Good/Feeling Good</u> text and workbook, by Kendall/Hunt Publishing Company, 1986

• Computer Labs (Apple II and Macintosh)

• Weight training facility

• Gymnasium and classroom

• VCR, TV monitors, and overhead projector

Procedures and Teaching Strategies

• cooperative learning activities are used to keep students on task and also to keep their interest levels high

• cognitive classroom activities are followed by gymnasium type lab activities which directly relate the two and result in a better learning situation

Program Description

HIGH SCHOOL FITNESS CONCEPTS
Required Semester Course

I. Unit Description

Designed to cover fundamental and current topics in physical fitness, diet and nutrition, and body composition maintenance. This semester course is established to encourage students to develop an individual optimum level of physical fitness, acquire knowledge of physical fitness concepts, and understand the significance of lifestyle on one's health and fitness.

II. Goals

The physical education program will provide all students with the opportunities to:

A. Develop an understanding of the effects of exercise on the human body through basic knowledge of current health related physical fitness concepts.

B. Develop positive social and emotional skills, attitudes, and behaviors to include consideration, cooperation, competition, and the acceptance of rules and authority.

C. Enhance their self concept through a sense of achievement and to become aware of their strengths and weaknesses, abilities, and limitations.

III. Objectives

A. The student will gain an understanding of individualized physical fitness as it relates to the health risk factors associated with premature death, and he or she will identify the benefits gained by exercising.

B. The student will understand health related and skill related fitness components and terminology.

C. The student will develop an understanding of the guidelines associated with exercise.

D. The student will understand the principles of training.

E. The student will understand the importance of maintaining acceptable standards of flexibility.

F. The student will gain an understanding of the components of cardiovascular fitness.

G. The student will understand the benefits gained from muscular fitness.

H. The student will understand the importance of maintaining proper body composition, weight control, and diet.

I. The student will gain an understanding of consumer issues related to fitness products, fraud, facilities, and advertising.

J. The student will know how to evaluate activities based on individual differences, personalities, social economic status, and physical abilities.

K. The student will be able to design their own physical fitness program.

IV. Unit Outline

A. Introduction
1. Trends in fitness
2. Attitudes toward physical fitness
3. Definition of physical fitness
4. Primary health risk factors
5. Benefits of exercise

B. Components of fitness
1. Health related fitness
2. Skill related fitness

C. Guidelines for exercise
1. Getting started
2. Helpful hints to success
3. Proper dress for exercise
4. Hot and cold weather conditions
5. Warming up and cooling down

D. Principles of training
1. Efficient and safe training
2. Principle of overload
3. Principle of progression
4. Principle of specificity

E. Flexibility
1. Definition
2. Importance
3. Types of stretching
4. Application of training principles
5. Safety precautions
6. Assessment
7. Exercise

F. Cardiovascular Fitness
1. Its importance
2. Circulatory and respiratory system
3. External methods of monitoring the heart
4. Cardiovascular disease
5. Benefits
6. Application of training principles
7. Assessment

G. Muscular Fitness
1. Muscular strength and endurance
2. Myths about weight training
3. Muscle fiber composition
4. Methods of developing muscular fitness
5. Application of training principles
6. Assessment
7. Weight training considerations
8. Muscular fitness exercises

H. Body composition, weight control, and diet
1. Body types
2. Body composition and assessment
3. Weight control
4. Weight loss, weight gain, and weight maintenance
5. Caloric cost of physical activities
6. Permanent weight control
7. Weight control misconceptions
8. Nutrition

I. Consumer issues
1. How to prevent getting "ripped off"
2. Learning how to be a knowledgeable consumer
3. The myth of spot reduction
4. False advertising claims
5. Drugs and weight control
6. Learning about health clubs
7. Advice on good and bad products

J. Evaluation of physical activities
1. Which activities are best
2. Categories of activities
3. Considerations before selecting activities

K. Designing your own program
1. Total fitness program
2. Making decisions about an individualized program
3. Starting a program
4. Program guidelines

V. Student Learner Outcomes/ Evaluation Method(s)

A. The student will define physical fitness, identify health risk factors, identify the benefits of exercise, and define body image.

Evaluation method:
Verbal and/or written–Test/worksheets

B. The student will identify the health related components of physical fitness, skill related components of physical fitness, describe the difference between health related and skill related components, and explain why the health related components of physical fitness are essential for all individuals.

Evaluation method:
Verbal and/or written–Test/worksheets

C. The student will identify factors to consider before engaging in a physical fitness program, identify precautions to be taken when exercising in extreme weather and/or environmental conditions, identify signs of heat illnesses caused by fluid loss, and describe the importance of warm-up and cool-down periods.

Evaluation method:
Teacher Observation
Verbal and/or written–Test/worksheets

D. The student will define and demonstrate the training principles of overload, progression, and specificity, and explain how overload is accomplished by varying the frequency, intensity, and time (duration).

Evaluation method:
Teacher Observation
Verbal and/or written–Test/worksheets

E. The student will identify health related problems associated with inadequate flexibility, describe and/or demonstrate how flexibility is improved through application of training principles, identify and/or demonstrate a variety of static and dynamic stretching activities that promote flexibility, describe and/or demonstrate safety procedures that should be followed when engaging in flexibility exercises, complete several self evaluation assessment tests of flexibility, and identify, describe, and/or demonstrate methods of determining levels of flexibility.

Evaluation method:
Teacher Observation
Verbal and/or written–Test/worksheets

F. The student will explain how the circulatory and respiratory systems are related to cardiovascular (CV) fitness, determine and/or demonstrate his/her target heart rate zone, identify health related problems associated with inadequate cardiovascular fitness, discuss the CV benefits of exercise, describe and/or demonstrate how CV fitness is improved through application of training principles, identify, describe, and/or demonstrate methods of determining levels of CV fitness, identify and participate in a variety of aerobic activities that promote CV fitness, complete several CV evaluation assessment tests, and describe and/or demonstrate safety procedures that should be followed when engaging in CV fitness activities.

Evaluation method:
Teacher Observation
Verbal and/or written–Test/worksheets

G. The student will identify benefits derived from participation in muscular fitness activities, identify myths commonly held about weight training, describe and/or demonstrate how muscular strength and muscular endurance are improved through application of training principles, identify, describe, and/or demonstrate methods of determining levels of muscular strength and endurance, identify health related problems associated with inadequate muscular strength and endurance, identify and demonstrate a variety of activities which promote muscular strength and endurance, and describe and demonstrate safety procedures which should be followed when engaging in muscular fitness activities.

Evaluation method:
Teacher Observation
Verbal and/or written–Test/worksheets

H. The student will describe three basic body types, define ideal body weight, overweight and obesity, describe four methods for testing body fat, identify medical problems associated with excessive body fat, explain why fat children and teenagers are more likely to be fat adults, describe weight loss, weight gain, and weight maintenance, complete a self evaluation body composition skin fold test and explain why permanent weight control is best achieved by a combination of diet and exercise.

Evaluation method:
Teacher Observation
Verbal and/or written–Test/worksheets

I. The student will differentiate between fact and fad, quackery and myths, as related to fitness, determine the validity of marketing claims promoting fitness products and services, identify consumer issues to product selection.

Evaluation method:
Verbal and/or written–Test/worksheets

J. The student shall describe the three categories of exercise and activities, identify the contributions of physical activities to the health related components of physical fitness, explain why health needs should be considered before selecting physical activities for an individual fitness program, explain why motor skills should be considered before selecting physical activities for an individual fitness program, and explain why financial considerations should be considered before selecting physical activities for an individual fitness program.

Evaluation method:
Verbal and/or written–Test/worksheets

K. The student will design and demonstrate personal fitness programs that will lead to or maintain optimal levels of flexibility, cardiovascular endurance, muscular strength, muscular endurance, and ideal body weight.

Evaluation method:
Teacher Observation
Verbal and/or written–Test/worksheets

L. The student will demonstrate an attitude that will contribute to the positive atmosphere of the class.

Evaluation method:
Teacher Observation

Each student is assessed in the five health related areas of fitness via the computerized Prudential Fitnessgram program. The Fitnessgram report card is mailed home so that parents can see the current health status of their child. A cover letter is mailed along with the Fitnessgram explaining the importance of maintaining at least a minimal level of fitness (Health Standard). Parents are encouraged to get involved in some form of family fitness activity.

Computerized progress reports are posted daily so students always know their current evaluation status. Student ID numbers are used instead of names to keep individual performance standards confidential.

Program Results

After the nine week unit is over, students are then given an opportunity to elect specific health related courses like stationary cycling, weight training, step aerobics, bicycle touring, walking/jogging, and tennis.

More and more students have elected physical education for enhancement, and the exercise facilities are being used during lunch periods and after school. Intramural and athletic programs have grown steadily over the last ten years. Many students have outside memberships at recreation centers and swim/tennis clubs.

Program Tips

Inform parents of this required course via a school open house and parent-teacher conference.

Guest speakers are used whenever possible to keep interest levels high. Hospital exercise physiologists, doctors, nurses, YMCA trained aerobics instructors, and chiropractors are asked to speak and lead class instruction. Investigate community resources and create opportunities for their involvement.

Challenged students work with their teachers to complete both lab and classroom assignments. Extra help is also available after school.

Extra credit assignments are available for students who desire to pursue a topic of interest or need to raise their grade point average.

Create support materials to complement the unit outline. The more senses involved in a learning situation, the better the result. Worksheets can accompany video presentations.

Investigate available resources and weave them into the curriculum where appropriate. Don't reinvent the wheel. (A complete listing of resources used in this program can be found at the end of this section.)

Personal Fitness Goal Setting Action Plan

Name: _____ Class _____

I. FUTURE DIRECTION

List three realistic goals that you could implement to help you improve your current health status. Look at your Fitnessgram and write your goals based on the performance of your three lowest criterion referenced standards of health.

1. _____

2. _____

3. _____

II. PRIORITIES

Using the above list, select your top two goals in order of importance.

1. _____

2. _____

III. THE MOST IMPORTANT PRIORITY

Select one of the above goals which you consider as the most important health related fitness priority for you, and one which you would really like to work on during the current semester of school. Write that goal below and set dates for starting towards and reaching that goal.

Goal _____

Target Dates: _____ Start _____ Completion _____

HELPS AND HINDRANCES

What will help you reach your goal? (Positive Forces)	What will stand in the way? (Negative Forces)
_____	_____
_____	_____
_____	_____
_____	_____

IV. HOW DO YOU GET THERE?

Establish a plan of action. Think about the people, steps, and dates you must consider to reach your goal. In order to design a sound personal fitness program you should follow specific steps. Steps in developing your personal fitness program are:

1. Evaluation–Look at your Fitnessgram and analyze your weak areas of fitness. What do you want to do, what can you do, and what will you do to start improving your current health related fitness?

2. Set short-term and long-term goals. Remember goals must be obtainable.

3. Select activities in which you will participate, by using the exercise programs and sports activities that you will like.

4. Periodically re-assess your fitness level by retaking the five health related Fitnessgram tests. Ask yourself, am I improving?

5. Don't give in or up. This problem is almost always mental and seldom physical.

6. Fight boredom with variety, exercise with friends and keep records.

Computing Your Target Heart Rate Zone

NAME _____ DATE_____ CLASS_____

Purpose: To identify a target heart rate zone which is a safe and comfortable level of overload that should be maintained to achieve a training effect.

Procedure: Study the example provided before completing this activity.

	EXAMPLE	FOR YOU LOWER LIMIT	UPPER LIMIT
START WITH 220 SUBTRACT YOUR AGE	220 -16	220 - _____	220 - _____
EQUALS MAXIMUM HEART RATE (MHR) MAXIMUM TIMES HEART SHOULD BEAT/MIN. SUBTRACT RESTING HEART RATE	204 -72	= _____ - _____	= _____ - _____
MULTIPLY BY: 60% – INACTIVE (Lower Limit) 90% – VERY ACTIVE (Safe Upper Limit)	132 X .60	_____ X .60	_____ X .90
ADD RESTING HEART RATE	79.20 +72	= _____ + _____	= _____ + _____
EQUALS TARGET HEART RATE (THR)	151 BEATS PER MINUTE		YOUR THR

TIP: When reproducing for classroom handouts, copy pages 140 and 141 back to back.

Working In Your Target Heart Range

NAME _____   DATE _____   CLASS _____

Purpose: To practice working in your target heart rate range by doing a walk/jog or stationary cycling workout.

Procedure: Provide answers to the following questions and graph your workout on the chart provided.

1. Draw a •••• line on the chart to represent your maximum heart rate. Write it down here _____.

2. Draw a —— line on the chart to represent the lower limit (60%) of your target heart rate zone. Write that number down here: _____.

3. Draw a ------- line on the chart to represent the upper limit (90%) of your target heart rate. Lightly shade in your target heart zone. Write your upper limit down here: _____.

4. What is your pre-exercise heart rate? _____ Mark it on the chart.

5. We will do a 30 minute workout. Try to stay within your THR zone. Record your heart rate at times listed below.

    HR after a 5 minute warmup: _____

    HR after 10 minutes of exercise: _____

    HR after 15 minutes of exercise: _____

    HR after 20 minutes of exercise: _____

    HR after 25 minutes of exercise: _____

    HR after a 5 minute cool down: _____

6. Graph a line showing how your heart rate progressed from normal conditions, through the warm-up, aerobic activity, cool-down and recovery. This line should correspond to the HR's taken in Number 5 above. Mark this line with a different color. Were you able to stay within your target heart rate range during the aerobic activity part of your workout? _____

TIP: When reproducing for classroom handouts, copy pages 140 and 141 back to back.

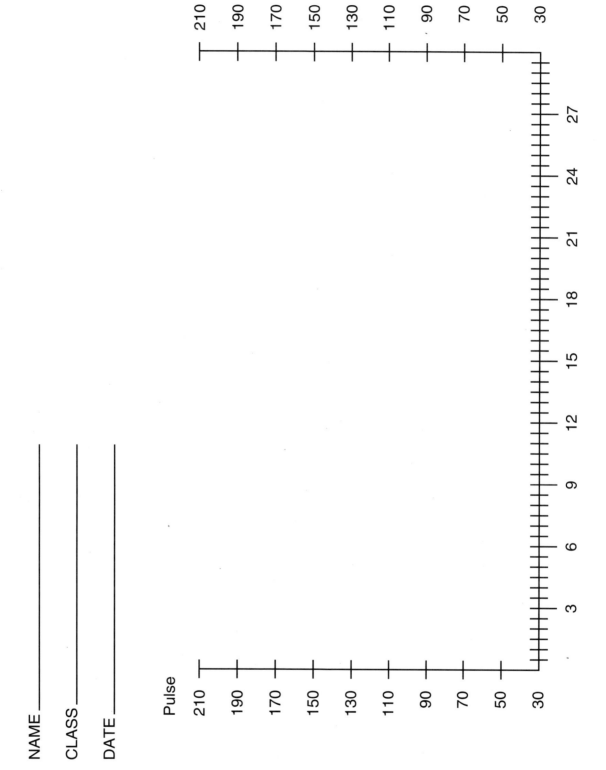

PULSE RATE CURVE

NAME
CLASS
DATE

Pulse

Benefits of Personal Fitness

NAME _____ DATE _____ CLASS _____

Purpose: To emphasize the physical and health benefits received from a personal fitness program.

1. Physical activity which contributes to all health related components of physical fitness can develop and maintain certain aspects of one's health. Identify three health problems less likely to occur as a result of a personal fitness program.

A. _____

B. _____

C. _____

2. With one (1) being most important and six (6) the least important, rank the following contributions of a personal fitness program, in terms of their importance to you.

_____A. Appearance   _____D. Health

_____B. Enjoyment and satisfaction   _____E. Relaxation

_____C. Slowing the aging process   _____F. More energy

3. As a result of participating in a personal fitness program, which of the following improvements would you expect in your appearance?

_____ Improved posture

_____ Muscle tone

_____ Efficient body movement

_____ Less fat tissue

_____ Improved complexion

4. List three goals of personal fitness you would like to achieve in the next three months.

A. _____

B. _____

C. _____

Identification of Quack Products

NAME_____ DATE_____ CLASS_____

Purpose: To become a more knowledgeable consumer.
Procedure: Complete the following activities.

1. Cut out one health, tanning spa, or fitness club advertisement and bring it to class for discussion.

2. Cut out one advertisement related to exercise and bring it to class for discussion. Use magazines or newspapers to find these advertisements.

3. Identify two examples of fat reduction exercise gadgets.

     1._____

     2._____

4. Ask three adults (parents, teachers or older friends) how they would go about losing weight from the stomach or buttocks.

     1. Name of adult: _____

     Response:_____

     2. Name of adult:_____

     Response:_____

     3. Name of adult: _____

     Response: _____

5. What would you do if someone started using a "Super Pill" which guaranteed a 15 pound loss in the first week?

Personal Fitness Notebook Requirements

Each notebook must include the following 3 sections, in the order listed below.

I. Goals Program
1. Health Related Test Results–Completed Fitnessgram
2. Goal Setting
3. Personal Fitness Program
4. Activity Plan

II. Newspaper and Magazine Articles:
1. You must have at least 5 health-related fitness articles from 5 different sources or dates. Articles must be about or related to:
   a. Flexibility
   b. Muscular Strength
   c. Muscular Endurance
   d. Cardiovascular Fitness
   e. Body Composition (Diet & Weight Control)

2. You must include a summary paragraph of each article, paraphrasing what you learned or read.

3. The articles must be neatly displayed.

III. Class Lecture Notes

Grading of Notebooks	Points
Fitness Goals Section	25
Articles and Summary	30
Class Lecture Notes	25
Neatness and Appearance	20
Total Notebook Points	100

PERSONAL FITNESS RESOURCE LIST

Resource Type:	Apple II & IBM Software
Resource Name:	**Physical Best**
Resource Description:	This comprehensive software lets you store test data, generate individual and group reports, manage the recognition system, and have more time for your students.
Health Related Topic	General Health Related Information
Vendor Name	AAHPERD
Vendor Address	1900 Association Drive
Vendor City	Reston, VA 22091

Resource Type:	Apple II Software
Resource Name:	**1 1/2 Mile Run Individual Exercise Prescription**
Resource Description:	This program develops an individual exercise prescription using the guidelines set forth by the American College of Sports Medicine. The individual enters age, weight, height, resting heart rate, and time for 1 1/2 mile run. The program calculates your test results, your physical fitness status, your aerobic fitness classification, your training program, interval training guidelines for running, sharpening your running suggestions, pacing yourself suggestions, and training tips.
Health Related Topic	Cardiovascular
Vendor Name	Human Factors Software
Vendor Address	3731 Dell Road
Vendor City	Carmichael, CA 95608

Resource Type:	Apple II Software
Resource Name:	**Aerobic Evaluation and Exercise Guidelines**
Resource Description:	This program develops an individual exercise prescription using the guidelines set forth by the American College of Sports Medicine. The individual enters age, weight, height, lifestyle, resting heart rate, and blood pressure. The program calculates exercise prescription, aerobic fitness classifications, your training intensity, keys to effective training, training frequency, basic caloric needs, your estimated caloric expenditures for several forms of exercise, and basic principles to observe.
Health Related Topic	Cardiovascular
Vendor Name	Human Factors Software
Vendor Address	3731 Dell Road
Vendor City	Carmichael, CA 95608

Resource Type:	Apple II Software
Resource Name:	**Cardiovascular Fitness Lab**
Resource Description:	An excellent program to explain the effects of exercise, smoking, stress on the heart. This program monitors your heart beat while exercising. Training hearts can be programmed into the computer and visual cues will indicate if the individual is able to exercise within the THR.
Health Related Topic	Cardiovascular
Vendor Name	HRM Software
Vendor Address	
Vendor City	Pleasantville, NY 10570

Resource Type:	Apple II Software
Resource Name:	**Fitnessgram**
Resource Description:	Fitnessgram is a youth fitness reporting system. It provides meaningful feedback to students, teachers, and parents following performance on a health related physical fitness assessment. The awards program is designed to emphasize exercise behavior.
Health Related Topic	General Health Related Information
Vendor Name	Institute for Aerobics Research
Vendor Address	12330 Preston Road
Vendor City	Dallas, TX 75230

Resource Type:	Apple II Software
Resource Name:	**Health Awareness Games**
Resource Description:	Innovative ways students can learn about their health status.
Health Related Topic	General Health Related Information
Vendor Name	HRM Software
Vendor Address	
Vendor City	Pleasantville, NY 10570

Resource Type:	Apple II Software
Resource Name:	**Health Risk Appraisal**
Resource Description:	Answer the questions and find out your current health risk for developing cancer, heart disease, stress related illnesses, and other hypokinetic illnesses.
Health Related Topic	General Health Related Information
Vendor Name	HRM Software
Vendor Address	
Vendor City	Pleasantville, NY 10570

Resource Type:	Apple II Software
Resource Name:	**Weight Training**
Resource Description:	This program estimates oxygen uptake and several metabolic parameters. The participant enters maximum lifts for nine different exercises and the computer will determine strength analysis which include % strength relative to body weight, progressive resistance training programs, and resistance relative to fitness level. Your program will also evaluate your caloric need and expenditure.
Health Related Topic	Muscle Strength & Endurance
Vendor Name	Human Factors Software
Vendor Address	3731 Dell Road
Vendor City	Carmichael, CA 95608

Resource Type:	Macintosh Software
Resource Name:	**Grade Busters: Making the Grade**
Resource Description:	Fast, reliable electronic gradebook that will save valuable time. Making the Grade saves all the information on 80 students per class with 160 assignments and 215 days attendance data in just 2.5 seconds. It permits up to ten assignment categories, which may be weighted into a single composite grade, or kept separate in a total points system.
Health Related Topic	Miscellaneous
Vendor Name	Jay Klein Productions
Vendor Address	1695 Summit Point Court
Vendor City	Colorado Springs, CO 80919

Resource Type: Macintosh Software
Resource Name: **MacDINE II**
Resource Description: This is a full-featured professional nutrition analysis program. You simply enter foods and exercise sessions by name or code. You can view the nutrient values of the food record. The program allows the user to select units of measure and will perform a food analysis for single or multiple days based on the measurement of calories, grams, % of calories, milligrams or % RDA. A Recipe Analysis feature makes planning diets, menus, meals simple.
Health Related Topic: Body Composition, Diet or Nutrition
Vendor Name: DINE Systems, Inc
Vendor Address: 586 North French Road, Suite 2
Vendor City: Amherst, NY 14228

Resource Type: Textbook
Resource Name: **Cooperation In The Classroom**
Resource Description: Great resource for developing cooperative learning activities in the gym and classroom.
Health Related Topic: Miscellaneous
Vendor Name: Interaction Book Company
Vendor Address: 7208 Cornelia Drive
Vendor City: Minneapolis, MN 55435

Resource Type: Textbook
Resource Name: **Experiments in Human Performance**
Resource Description: Supplemental text
Health Related Topic: General Health Related Information
Vendor Name: WM. C. Brown Publishers
Vendor Address: 2460 Kerper Boulevard
Vendor City: Dubuque, IA 52001

Resource Type: Textbook
Resource Name: **Fitness Facts: The Healthy Living Handbook**
Resource Description: Supplemental text
Health Related Topic: General Health Related Information
Vendor Name: Human Kinetics Publishers, Inc.
Vendor Address: P.O. Box 5076
Vendor City: Champaign, IL 61825-5076

Resource Type: Textbook
Resource Name: **Fitness For Life**
Resource Description: Supplemental text
Health Related Topic: General Health Related Information
Vendor Name: Scott, Foresman and Company
Vendor Address: 1900 Lake Street
Vendor City: Evanston, IL 60201

Resource Type: Textbook
Resource Name: **Fitness Leaders Handbook**
Resource Description: Supplemental text
Health Related Topic: General Health Related Information
Vendor Name: Human Kinetics Publishers, Inc.
Vendor Address: P.O. Box 5076
Vendor City: Champaign, IL 61825-5076

Resource Type:	Textbook
Resource Name:	**Kid Fitness: A Complete Shape-up Program**
Resource Description:	Supplemental text
Health Related Topic	General Health Related Information
Vendor Name	Bantam Books
Vendor Address	666 Fifth Avenue
Vendor City	New York, NY 10103

Resource Type:	Textbook
Resource Name:	**Lifetime Physical Fitness and Wellness**
Resource Description:	Supplemental text
Health Related Topic	General Health Related Information
Vendor Name	Morton Publishing Company
Vendor Address	925 W. Kenyon Ave. – Unit 12
Vendor City	Englewood, CO 80110

Resource Type:	Textbook
Resource Name:	**Personal Fitness and You**
Resource Description:	Supplemental text
Health Related Topic	General Health Related Information
Vendor Name	Hunter Textbooks Inc.
Vendor Address	823 Reynolda Road
Vendor City	Winston-Salem, NC 27104

Resource Type:	Textbook
Resource Name:	**Personal Fitness: Looking Good Feeling Good**
Resource Description:	This is the primary textbook used in this course. Each student has his/her own hardbound text. Each teacher has a Teachers Edition and students do lab experiments from an Activity Handbook.
Health Related Topic	General Health Related Information
Vendor Name	Kendall/Hunt Publishing Company
Vendor Address	4050 Westmark Drive
Vendor City	Dubuque, IA 52002

Resource Type:	Textbook
Resource Name:	**Physical Best Educational Kit**
Resource Description:	This kit gives you the program materials you need to add a fitness emphasis to your physical education curriculum or to create an independent program. Written for grades K-6 and 6-12, it will help you teach students fitness basics that will last a lifetime. Kit includes the Instructor's Guide, teaching ideas cards, methods of integrating a recognition system, plus reproducible samples of key elements of the Physical Best Program.
Health Related Topic	General Health Related Information
Vendor Name	AAHPERD
Vendor Address	1900 Association Drive
Vendor City	Reston, VA 22091

Resource Type:	Textbook
Resource Name:	**Principles and Labs for Physical Fitness & Wellness**
Resource Description:	Supplemental text
Health Related Topic	General Health Related Information
Vendor Name	Morton Publishing Company
Vendor Address	925 W. Kenyon Ave. – Unit 12
Vendor City	Englewood, CO 80110

Resource Type:	Textbook
Resource Name:	**The Aerobics Program For Total Well Being**
Resource Description:	Supplemental text
Health Related Topic	General Health Related Information
Vendor Name	M. Evansand Company, Inc.
Vendor Address	216 East 49 Street
Vendor City	New York, NY 10017

Resource Type:	Textbook
Resource Name:	**Wellness: Exercise and Physical Fitness**
Resource Description:	Supplemental text
Health Related Topic	General Health Related Information
Vendor Name	The Dushkin Publishing Group, Inc.
Vendor Address	
Vendor City	Guilford, CT 06437

Resource Type:	Video Tape
Resource Name:	**Cycling Warm-up Exercise Shorts**
Resource Description:	This video leads students through a series of warm-up exercises prior to doing a cycling activity.
Health Related Topic	Warm-up exercises
Vendor Name	Karl Lorimar Home Video
Vendor Address	See your local video rental store
Vendor City	

Resource Type:	Video Tape
Resource Name:	**Fat Chance in a Thin World**
Resource Description:	This video is from the Nova Series on Public Television and it is one of the best films made on the discussion of why and how humans get fat.
Health Related Topic	Body Composition, Diet or Nutrition
Vendor Name	PBS Home Video
Vendor Address	See your local video rental store
Vendor City	

Resource Type:	Video Tape
Resource Name:	**Fit or Fat For the '90s**
Resource Description:	The dynamic and entertaining author of the phenomenal bestseller, *Fit or Fat?* shares his scientific expertise on losing the fat without losing health. Covert Baily lays out all the latest discoveries in nutritional science in a clear, entertaining and practical way. You'll laugh with Covert as he teaches you how eating right and exercise can be not only enjoyable, but easy.
Health Related Topic	General Health Related
Vendor Name	1991 Pacific Arts Video Publishing
Vendor Address	11858 La Grange Ave.
Vendor City	Los Angeles, CA 90025

Resource Type:	Video Tape
Resource Name:	**Health Walking Training System**
Resource Description:	The Nike-SyberVision Health Walking System includes two audio cassettes, a 60-minute video and a study guide. The video shows you proper walking techniques and the study guide provides you with a journal in which you can record your progress. Health Walking provides you with a comprehensive plan that not only teaches you the most beneficial way to walk but provides the tools to transform you from a sedentary person to a mobile, high-energy person.
Health Related Topic	General Health Related Information
Vendor Name	SyberVision Systems Inc.
Vendor Address	7133 Knoll Center Parkway
Vendor City	Pleasanton, CA 94566

Resource Type:	Video Tape
Resource Name:	**Jacki Sorensen's Aerobic Dancing**
Resource Description:	Jacki Sorensen leads this aerobic dance tape. Connecting two or three monitors together will help students follow the routines.
Health Related Topic	Cardiovascular
Vendor Name	Video Cassette Inc.
Vendor Address	
Vendor City	Universal City, CA 91608

Resource Type:	Video Tape
Resource Name:	**Jogging Warm-Up Exercise Shorts**
Resource Description:	This video leads students through a series of warm-up exercises prior to doing a jogging activity.
Health Related Topic	Warm-up exercises
Vendor Name	Karl Lorimer Home Videos
Vendor Address	See your local video rental store
Vendor City	

Resource Type:	Video Tape
Resource Name:	**Keys to Weight Training**
Resource Description:	This video leads the viewers through three progressively challenging free weight routines and a selection of effective machine exercises. Includes correct and safe lifting techniques to improve overall body conditioning, strength and flexibility, and cardiovascular development.
Health Related Topic	General Health Related Information
Vendor Name	Cambridge Physical Education & Health
Vendor Address	P.O. Box 2153, Dept. PE9
Vendor City	Charleston, WV 25238-2153

Resource Type:	Video Tape
Resource Name:	**Measuring Body Fat Using Skinfolds**
Resource Description:	Dr. Lohman explains and demonstrates how to measure body fat using the skinfold caliper method. The tape shows how to select reliable calipers, take measurements, and evaluate test results. This video comes with body fat norms to compare students' measurements with the national norms for 6- to 18-year-olds.
Health Related Topic	Body Composition, Diet or Nutrition
Vendor Name	Human Kinetics Publishers, Inc.
Vendor Address	P.O. Box 5076
Vendor City	Champaign, IL 61825-5076

Resource Type:	Video Tape
Resource Name:	**Muscle Fibre**
Resource Description:	In-depth film discussing the type of muscle fibres and their function in humans and animals. Excellent film to introduce the concepts of muscular strength and endurance.
Health Related Topic	Muscular Strength & Endurance
Vendor Name	New Dimension Films
Vendor Address	
Vendor City	Eugene, OR 97401

Resource Type:	Video Tape
Resource Name:	**My Heart Your Heart**
Resource Description:	Documentary of Jim Lear, of the public television Lear-McNeil Report, and how heart disease changed his life.
Health Related Topic	Cardiovascular
Vendor Name	See your local video store
Vendor Address	
Vendor City	

Resource Type:	Video Tape
Resource Name:	**Oh My Aching Back**
Resource Description:	A comprehensive and educational program that covers the complete spectrum of back problems and the rehabilitation and prevention of back injuries. The tape includes: commentary from orthopedic surgeons, as well as exercise routines for keeping your back strong, flexible and trouble free.
Health Related Topic	Flexibility
Vendor Name	Champions on Films
Vendor Address	745 State Circle, P.O. Box 1941
Vendor City	Ann Arbor, MI 48108

Resource Type:	Video Tape
Resource Name:	**Power Stepping with Lynne Brick**
Resource Description:	Power stepping is a fun and effective way to work out the entire class. Aerobic steps are needed. Connecting two or three monitors together will help students follow the routines.
Health Related Topic	Cardiovascular
Vendor Name	Power Productions International Inc.
Vendor Address	18217 Flower Hill Way, Suite A
Vendor City	Gaithersburg, MD 20879

Resource Type:	Video Tape
Resource Name:	**Progressive Resistance Exercise**
Resource Description:	This video explains and demonstrates the various types of progressive resistance exercises used today. Safety precautions, muscle groups, proper spotting, and lifting techniques are discussed and demonstrated.
Health Related Topic	Muscular Strength & Endurance
Vendor Name	Dr. Andy Ertl
Vendor Address	University of California–Davis
Vendor City	Davis, CA 95616

Resource Type:	Video Tape
Resource Name:	**Ropics–Rope Jumping Redefined**
Resource Description:	A jumping program to solve the problems of early exhaustion, shin splints and calf soreness which plague the traditional approach. Video includes step-by-step instruction on 15 basic and intermediate level techniques. It illustrates a complete class for beginners and an intermediate level workout.
Health Related Topic	Cardiovascular
Vendor Name	Cambridge Physical Education and Health
Vendor Address	P.O. Box 2153–Dept. PE9
Vendor City	Charleston, WV 25328-2153

Resource Type:	Video Tape
Resource Name:	**Shape Up with Arnold**
Resource Description:	Arnold Schwartzenegger demonstrates how to lift weight correctly and safely. Rachel McLish and Arnold use both free weight and machine lifting techniques in this demonstration video. A beginners program and advanced male and female program are included in the video.
Health Related Topic	Muscular Strength & Endurance
Vendor Name	Michael Linder Productions
Vendor Address	Video Associates, Inc.
Vendor City	Hollywood, CA 90028

Resource Type:	Video Tape
Resource Name:	**Stretching to Prevent Muscle-Related Injuries**
Resource Description:	This video presents a complete body stretching program from the ankles to the neck and includes several exercises to help prevent back problems.
Health Related Topic	Flexibility
Vendor Name	Cambridge Physical Education and Health
Vendor Address	P.O. Box 2153–Dept. PE9
Vendor City	Charleston, WV 25328-2153

Resource Type:	Video Tape
Resource Name:	**The New Best of Bodies in Motion**
Resource Description:	An excellent exercise video for students to do in a class setting. Connecting two or three monitors together will help students follow the routines.
Health Related Topic	Muscular Strength & Endurance
Vendor Name	JCI Video
Vendor Address	See your local video rental store
Vendor City	Woodland Hills, CA 91367

Resource Type:	Video Tape
Resource Name:	**The Walk America Video**
Resource Description:	A documentary video of Rob Sweetgall's 50-state walk across America. Excellent video to motivate students and adults to walk for exercise.
Health Related Topic	Cardiovascular
Vendor Name	Creative Walking, Inc.
Vendor Address	8230 Forsyth Blvd
Vendor City	St. Louis, MO 63105

Personal Fitness Course

Organization: Florida Department of Education
Room 414, Florida Education Center
325 West Gaines Street
Tallahassee, FL 32399-0400

Phone: (904) 488-7835

Contributor: Manny Harageones–Physical Activity Specialist

Program Objective

• to provide students with opportunities to develop an individual optimal level of physical fitness, acquire knowledge of physical fitness concepts, and understand the significance of lifestyle on one's health and fitness

Program Description

In 1983, Florida became the first state to develop and implement a required fitness concepts course for high school graduation. This fitness education program has been modeled by many states, school districts, and individual schools in the country. Following is the revised 1992 version of the state adopted Florida Department of Education student performance standards for the Personal Fitness course.

COURSE STUDENT PERFORMANCE STANDARDS

After successfully completing this course, the student will:

1. Understand and apply safety practices.

The student will:

- describe and demonstrate safety procedures which should be followed when engaging in flexibility, cardiovascular, muscular strength, and muscular endurance activities.

- explain methods of maintaining proper fluid balance during physical activity.

- identify signs of heat illnesses caused by fluid loss.

- identify precautions to be taken when exercising in extreme weather and/or environmental conditions.

2. Assess individual fitness levels.

The student will:

- identify methods of determining level of flexibility.

- identify methods of determining level of cardiovascular fitness.

- identify methods of determining level of muscular strength and muscular endurance.

- identify methods of determining estimated percent of body fat.

- define ideal body weight.

- describe at least one method of determining level of flexibility.

- describe at least one method of determining level of cardiovascular fitness.

- describe at least one method of determining level of muscular strength and muscular endurance.

- describe at least one method of determining estimated percent of body fat.

- describe at least one method of determining ideal body weight.

3. Understand and interpret health-related fitness assessment results.

The student will:

• identify and interpret his/her level of flexibility, cardiovascular fitness, muscular strength, muscular endurance, and percentage of body fat in relation to criterion-referenced health fitness standards.

4. Set specific and realistic health-related fitness goals.

The student will:

• set short-term, intermediate, and long-term goals based on health-related fitness assessment results.

5. Understand the components of physical fitness.

The student will:

• define physical fitness.

• identify and describe each of the health-related components of physical fitness.

• identify and describe each of the skill-related components of physical fitness.

• compare and differentiate between health-related fitness and skill-related fitness.

6. Understand health problems associated with inadequate fitness levels.

The student will:

• identify health related problems associated with inadequate flexibility.

• identify health related problems associated with inadequate cardiovascular fitness.

• identify health related problems associated with inadequate muscular strength and muscular endurance.

• identify health related problems associated with an abnormal percentage of body fat.

7. Understand the relationship between physical fitness activities and stress.

The student will:

• define stress.

• identify the different types of stress.

• identify the positive and negative effects of stress.

• identify specific health problems that may be caused or affected by negative stress.

• identify stressful events in daily life.

• identify positive coping strategies.

• identify negative coping strategies.

• identify techniques of progressive relaxation.

• describe the benefits of vigorous and nonvigorous physical activities to stress diversion.

8. Evaluate physical activities in terms of fitness value.

The student will:

• identify the contributions of physical activities to the development of the health-related components of physical fitness.

• identify the contributions of physical activities to stress diversion.

9. Select from a variety of activities which will improve health-related physical fitness.

The student will:

• identify a variety of static and dynamic stretching exercises which promote flexibility.

• identify a variety of aerobic activities which promote cardiovascular fitness.

• identify a variety of activities which promote muscular strength and muscular endurance.

• identify a variety of activities which promote ideal body weight.

• identify a variety of activities which promote stress diversion.

10. Design a fitness program that meets individual needs and interests.

The student will:

• design a personal fitness program that will lead to or maintain an optimal level of health-related fitness based on an understanding of training principles, individual fitness and skill level, personal goals, and availability of resources.

11. Understand and apply correct biomechanical and physiological principles related to exercise and training.

The student will:

• identify factors one should consider before engaging in a physical fitness program.

• describe the importance of a warm-up/cool-down period when participating in physical activity.

• describe the training principles of overload, progression, and specificity (frequency, intensity, duration).

• describe how flexibility is improved through application of the training principles.

• identify the biomechanical principles related to flexibility activities.

• describe how cardiovascular fitness is improved through application of the training principles.

• identify the biomechanical principles related to cardiovascular activities.

• describe how muscular strength and muscular endurance are improved through application of the training principles.

• identify the biomechanical principles related to muscular strength and muscular endurance activities.

• determine the range of target heart rate zone.

12. Exhibit an improved level of health-related physical fitness.

The student will:

• demonstrate an improvement of the health-related components of physical fitness.

13. Assess individual lifestyles.

The student will:

• identify the primary risk factors associated with disease, disability, and premature death.

• differentiate between changeable and unchangeable risk factors.

• identify risk factors that need to be reduced or modified to pursue a healthy lifestyle.

• describe the relationship between health and fitness and lifestyle.

14. Understand sound nutritional practices related to physical fitness.

The student will:

• identify facts and fallacies associated with nutritional practices related to physical activity.

• explain the use of exercise as a method of weight control.

• explain the use of diet as a method of weight control.

• explain the combined use of exercise and diet as a method of weight control.

15. Understand consumer issues related to physical fitness.

The student will:

• differentiate among fact, fad, quackery, and fallacies as related to fitness.

• determine the validity of marketing claims promoting fitness products and services.

• identify consumer issues related to selection, purchase, care and maintenance of personal fitness equipment.

• identify the dangers associated with the use of performance-altering drugs (e.g. steroids).

16. Understand the values derived from participation in physical fitness activities.

The student will:

• identify attitudes that people have towards exercise and physical activities.

• identify reasons why fitness should be a compelling state and national concern.

• describe the benefits of participating in a regular personal fitness program.

• describe the benefits of achieving optimal fitness.

Program Support Materials

A two-fold brochure entitled "What Every Parent Should Know About Florida's High School Physical Education" was created to answer any questions and explain the changes in more detail. The body of the text follows.

There Have Been Some Changes Made In Physical Education

High school physical education is not what you knew when you went to school. The old "P.E." or "gym" had a good purpose, to exercise young bodies so they would grow stronger and healthier. The changes in Florida's program go far beyond that. The purpose now is to assist students in acquiring the skills, knowledge, and motivation to incorporate physical activity into their daily lives.

Prevention is the key to good health and being physically active is a key for prevention. The role of physical activity in promoting good health and reducing the likelihood of disease is becoming increasingly clear. As research evidence continues to mount and the relationship between physical activity and health becomes clearer, it is critical that schools help students develop competencies for an active lifestyle. Florida's high school physical education program offers a variety of courses focusing on lifelong physical activities.

"There is a close relationship between physical health and mental health. Students who are fit not only receive the physical benefits, but are in better shape to learn their lessons in school. Since learning is the primary goal of education, it is extremely important that physical education be an integral part of the overall curriculum."

Betty Castor
Commissioner of Education

Physical Education Courses

Florida's high school physical education program provides students with opportunities to select courses according to their interests. No individual school is expected to offer all physical education courses. It is recommended that each school evaluate its available facilities and the competencies of its instructional staff to determine possible course offerings. It is further recommended that each school survey its students to determine their interests.

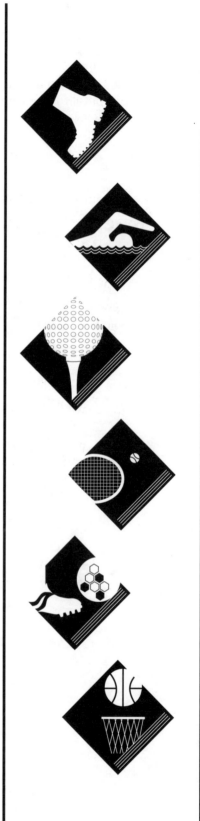

Fitness

- –Personal Fitness
- –Beginning Weight Training
- –Intermediate Weight Training
- –Advanced Weight Training
- –Beginning Power Weight Training
- –Fitness Lifestyle Design
- –Fitness Issues for Adolescence
- –Beginning Aerobics
- –Intermediate Aerobics
- –Advanced Aerobics
- –Comprehensive Fitness

Individual and Dual

- –Beginning Gymnastics
- –Intermediate Gymnastics
- –Advanced Gymnastics
- –Beginning Swimming
- –Advanced Swimming
- –Water Safety
- –Beginning Tennis
- –Intermediate Tennis
- –Advanced Tennis
- –Beginning Golf
- –Intermediate Golf
- –Paddleball/Racquetball/ Handball
- –Beginning Racquetball
- –Intermediate Racquetball
- –Beginning Wrestling
- –Intermediate Wrestling
- –Self Defense Activities
- –Recreational Activities
- –Outdoor Education
- –Care & Prevention of Athletic Injuries
- –Individual and Dual Sports I
- –Individual and Dual Sports II
- –Individual and Dual Sports III

Team

- –Track and Field
- –Basketball
- –Soccer
- –Softball
- –Beginning Volleyball
- –Intermediate Volleyball
- –Team Sports I
- –Team Sports II
- –Sports Officiating

Adaptive

- –Adaptive Physical Education I.E.P.
- –Individual Sports for Disabled Students
- –Team Sports for Disabled Students
- –Recreational Activities for Disabled Students
- –Aquatics for Disabled Students

Personal Fitness Course

The Personal Fitness Course is Florida's physical education high school graduation requirement. The purpose of the course is to provide students with opportunities to develop an individual optimal level of physical fitness, acquire knowledge of physical fitness concepts, and understand the significance of lifestyle on one's health and fitness.

The content of the course includes:

–Knowledge of the importance of physical fitness

–Assessment of flexibility, cardiovascular fitness, muscular strength and endurance, and body composition

–Knowledge of health problems associated with inadequate fitness levels

–Knowledge and application of biomechanical and physiological principles to improve and maintain the health-related components of physical fitness

–Knowledge of safety practices associated with physical fitness

–Knowledge of psychological values of physical fitness including stress management

–Knowledge of sound nutritional practices related to physical fitness

–Knowledge of consumer issues related to physical fitness

What You Can Do About High School Physical Education

Parents who are interested in helping improve the physical fitness and health of their children can work with their school in many ways. For instance:

–Learn the details of your school's physical education program and find ways to strengthen physical education activities.

–Work to make sure your school has adequate facilities and equipment.

–When you visit your school, make a point to talk with physical education instructors and see what you can do specifically for your child.

–Encourage your child to exercise regularly and eat sensibly.

–Arrange for more physical activities that involve the entire family-hiking, cycling or swimming.

–Apply the same principles in your own life. You'll live better for it!

Office of Physical Activity
Florida Department of Education
Room 414, Florida Education Center
325 West Gaines Street
Tallahassee, Florida 32399-0400
904/488-7835

Personal Improvement Plan—P.I.P.

School: Bellehaven Elementary School
4401 Free Pike Drive
Dayton, OH 45416
Phone: (513) 276-2141
Contributor: Keith M. Cosby

Program Objectives

- to improve students' fitness levels in accordance with AAHPERD assessment instruments

- to help students to understand they have the ability to improve their fitness scores

Materials/Equipment Needed

- taped music – two (2) minute increments

- tape player

- gymnasium (or recreation area)

- four (4) poster boards

- four (4) markers

- four (4) traffic cones

- jump rope for each student

- optional: pull-up bars and climbing ropes

Procedures and Teaching Strategies

- allow student input when determining activities for each station

- method to incorporate fitness into physical education lessons every day

Program Description

The Personal Improvement Plan consists of four (4) components which correspond to the Physical Best fitness program.

1. Cardiovascular Endurance Building

2. Upper Body Endurance Building

3. Abdominal Endurance Building

4. Flexibility

Make four (4) posters and title each with one of the elements listed above. Allow the students to come up with activities they can do in the gym to work on these specific parts of their body. For example, jogging, jumping rope, or power walking could be listed on the "Cardiovascular Endurance Building" poster. Edit the posters down to no more than eight (8) activities per poster.

Display the posters on the walls in order. Before class begins, the students pick one (1) activity from each of the first three (3) posters. When the music begins, they start with an activity from Poster #1. The students do that activity until the music changes. They then move on to an activity from Poster #2 and work on that activity until the music changes. They do the same with Poster #3. Poster #4 lists five (5) required stretches that students will do until the music stops.

This activity is used before each class and incorporates fitness into the lessons every day. It is also good fitness practice for the Physical Best testing program.

SAMPLE POSTERS

1. Cardiovascular – jogging, power walking, rope skipping, jogging in place

2. Upper Body Endurance – wall push-ups, pull-ups, push-ups, jumping rope, arm sprints (climbing rope)

3. Abdominal Endurance – bent knee sit-ups, crunches, V-ups

4. Flexibility – list five (5) stretches

Program Results

This method was an easy and consistent way to practice the fitness components of the Physical Best program. Students noted improvement on their test scores and experienced ownership in their improvement.

Program Tips

Homework – have students design a P.I.P. with mom, dad, sister, or brother.

Physical Management

School: Niles West High School
5701 Oakton
Skokie, IL 60077
Phone: (708) 966-3800
Contributor: Judi Sloan–ILLINOIS TEACHER OF THE YEAR

Program Objectives

• to offer students with weight control problems an alternative to regular physical education classes

• to create an awareness of how the physical education teacher can play an important role in the treatment of adolescent obesity

Materials/Equipment Needed

• physical education instructor

• gymnasium (or recreation area)

• classroom setting

• proper flooring for aerobic exercise activities

• fitness assessment equipment

• equipment for a variety of fitness activities

Procedures and Teaching Strategies

• introduce a school based intervention program in physical education which utilizes exercise, nutrition and behavior modification

• make the class attractive to students who feel uncomfortable in the regular physical education setting and to those who would like help in working on lifestyle change

• students perform better due to the non-threatening environment

• utilize success-oriented structured activities

• work with the guidance department, school nurses, and experts outside the school

Program Description

Physical Management consists of physical activity, behavior modification and nutrition education centered upon the theme of helping students to manage themselves better, especially in terms of weight control. Besides providing structured activity opportunities geared toward the participants, there is a great deal of encouragement and incentive to participate during non-school hours. In addition to administering the program, the physical education teacher will work with the guidance department, school nurse, and experts outside the school. The program is offered each semester and is open to all students who qualify by recommendation of the counselor, physical education staff, or other professionals.

Without this program, students with weight control problems must take the regular physical education class offerings or adaptive physical education. That is a problem for these students because of the social and emotional problems associated with being overweight. Ridicule coupled with poor performance in the activities of the regular setting create a negative experience daily.

For the best possible learning environment, students should be separated by gender. There are times when certain activities lend to coed participation, but more gains are made when the classes meet separately. Overweight boys and girls have a difficult time handling social problems of adolescence, thus separation by gender is critical.

Generally obese children and adolescents tend to experience social and psychological problems. These young people have poor body image and low self-concept. Many times the ridicule and isolation result in a child who is unwilling to participate in physical activity and who exhibits poor motor skills. This creates a vicious cycle of inactivity, greater obesity, and further inactivity.

Course Materials

In this particular class, the Physical Education uniform is required only if it fits comfortably. The student may choose another shirt, shorts, or sweats to be worn as clothes for class if there is a problem with fit. Each student must have a three ring folder for class.

Teaching Materials

A heavy emphasis on nutrition and behavior modification is essential. Guest lecturers and special video material including films and cassettes are utilized during the course. The students will be required to keep notebooks of hand-out materials and records of their progress in exercise and nutrition. The following are reference materials used in the course.

Association for Research and Professional Councils and Societies (1983).

Corbin, C.B. and Lindsey, R. (1983) Fitness for Life: Glenview, Scott, Foresman and Co.

Hockey, R.V., (1989) Physical Fitness, The Pathway to Healthful Living: St. Louis, Times Mirror/Mosley College Publishing.

Implementation of Health Fitness Exercise Programs: Reston, AAHPERD.

Jacobsen, M. and Fritechner, S. (1986). The Fast Food Guide: New York, Workmans Publishing Co. Inc.

Lyone, P., and Burgant, D. (1989) Great Shape-The First Exercise Book for Large Women: New York, Arbor House, William Morrows and Co. Inc.

Merkin., Gabe (1983). Getting Thin: Boston, Little, Brown and Co.

Roberts, Nancy (1985) Breaking All the Rules: New York, Viking Penguin, Inc.

William, C., Harogeones, E., Johnson, D., and Smith, C. (1986). Personal Fitness: Looking Good/Feeling Good. Dubuque, Kendall/Hunt Publishing Co.

Course Outcomes

GOAL 1: As a result of their schooling, students will be able to understand the physical development, structure and functions of the human body.

1. Understand the effects of various kinds of strength training.

2. Evaluate personal strength, flexibility, aerobic capacity and the influence of exercise.

3. Understand the effects of adequate body strength, muscular endurance, flexibility, and aerobic capacity on the body.

4. Know physical endurance events, strength events, and flexibility activities commensurate to an appropriate training level.

5. Understand the effects of nutrition and drugs on performance.

GOAL 2: As a result of their schooling, students will be able to understand principles of nutrition, exercise, efficient management of emotional stress, positive self-concept development, drug use and abuse, and the prevention of illness.

1. Understand principles of a training program for development and maintenance of cardiorespiratory endurance, muscular strength and endurance, and flexibility.

2. Know the comparative energy expenditure of selected physical activities.

3. Identify a training program for improving body composition.

4. Understand the influences of physical activity on stress control.

5. Identify coping mechanisms for controlling stress.

6. Understand the influences of stress on performance of selected sports and activities.

7. Understand the critical aspects of quality nutrition, food groups, serving requirements, and variety.

GOAL 3: As a result of their schooling, students will be able to understand consumer health and safety including environmental health.

1. Wear appropriate clothing and footwear while performing physical activities.

2. Perform with appropriate safety equipment in safe environments.

3. Know the importance of proper size and construction design in selecting various sports and fitness products.

GOAL 4: As a result of their schooling, students will be able to demonstrate basic skills and physical fitness necessary to participate in a variety of conditioning exercises or leisure activities such as sports and dance. By the end of grade 10, students should be able to:

1. Sustain an aerobic activity for a specified period of time appropriate to their developmental stage.

2. Perform exercises for strength development for a specified number of repetitions appropriate to their developmental stage.

3. Perform static stretches for a specified time appropriate to their developmental stage.

4. Perform activity sequences requiring cardiorespiratory efficiency.

5. Perform a variety of activity sequences requiring flexibility.

6. Perform a variety of activity sequences requiring muscular strength and endurance.

7. Identify several principles of growth and development that affect performance.

8. Perform an appropriate progression of skills in selected physical activities.

9. Know the effects of exercise on metabolism, heart disease, and hypertension.

10. Develop and maintain cardio-respiratory strength and endurance.

11. Develop and maintain muscular-skeletal strength and endurance.

12. Develop and maintain coordination and dexterity.

13. Understand the history, etiquette, equipment, terminology, rules and scoring, technique and strategy of various sporting activities.

GOAL 5: As a result of their schooling, students will be able to plan a personal physical fitness and health program.

1. Know the relationship between diet and exercise in controlling body composition.

GOAL 6: As a result of their schooling, students will be able to perform a variety of complex motor activities.

1. Apply rules of individual/dual sports.

2. Perform several individual/dual sports and demonstrate correct skills and position during play.

3. Demonstrate knowledge of rules in selected individual sports and self-testing events.

4. Keep body under control while performing.

5. Demonstrate the transfer of skills and/or strategies of one activity to another similar activity.

GOAL 7: As a result of their schooling, students will be able to identify behaviors and learn strategies to help them be successful.

1. Develop an understanding for caloric balance, i.e., calories in versus calories out.

2. Understand the pressures of media advertising.

3. Learn good snacking habits, including reduction of high calorie, low nutrition treats.

4. Identify behaviors which negatively effect weight control, such as speed of eating, chronic second portions, high calorie choices of intake.

5. Learn strategies for more functional activity, such as walking, bicycling, and jogging.

6. Identify cues which lead to inactivity, i.e., watching TV, lying down after school to nap, selecting friends who are inactive.

GOAL 8: As a result of their schooling, students will be able to demonstrate positive social interaction especially during stressful competitive situations.

1. Students will apply the rules of the game without regard to score.

2. Students will demonstrate humility in winning and grace in defeat.

3. Students will demonstrate acceptance of one another without regard to physical ability.

COURSE OUTLINE FOR TWO (2) SEMESTERS

Classroom Phase ―――――――――――――――――――――――――――

FIRST SEMESTER

Week 1-6

1. Define physical fitness.

2. Identify health risk factors.

3. Understand benefits of exercise.

4. Identify skill related components of physical fitness.

5. Understand the relationship of health and scores on fitness tests.

6. Work on one behavior modification each week which relates specifically to exercise.

7. Do "Getting to Know You" activities.

8. Emphasize the use of exercise as an important factor in changing and maintaining healthy body composition.

Week 7-12

1. Review guidelines for exercise.

2. Define the training principles of overload:

   a. Frequency

   b. Intensity

   c. Duration

3. Define principles of progression.

4. Define principle of specificity.

5. Continue working on one new behavior modification each week, but begin to add eating changes.

6. Begin to use log sheets for use in outside of class exercise programs.

Week 13-18

1. Define obesity.

2. Explain creeping obesity.

3. Explain principles of healthy weight loss and weight gain.

4. Discuss principles of weight maintenance/permanent weight control.

5. Distinguish the correlation between fat grams and calories.

6. Correlate good nutrition and healthy weight loss to the unhealthy promises of fad diets.

7. Continue with behavior modification.

8. Continue with the exercise logs.

SECOND SEMESTER

Week 19-24

1. Begin marking good intake.

2. Continue with behavior modification techniques.

3. Understand how to read labels.

4. Teach goal setting and planning ahead.

5. Discuss the art of grocery shopping.

6. Demonstrate and show examples of healthy cooking.

7. Discuss how to pack good lunches.

8. Discuss effects of fast foods.

9. Continue exercise log.

Week 25-30

1. Talk about body image.

2. Work on self concept and self esteem.

3. Have a fashion consultant come in and discuss fashion for the large man or woman.

4. Work on hair care and make-up.

5. Discuss and practice assertive behavior.

6. Discuss accepting responsibility for all decisions and actions.

7. Identify personal individual priorities.

8. Continue exercise log and food log.

Week 31-36

1. Begin to have classroom every other week as the opportunity arises to do more outdoor physical activities.

2. Schedule a trip to the Teams Course as a field trip.

3. Use class evaluation sheets to enhance class discussion on course improvements.

4. Work on a summer program for underclass students.

Activity Phase

The activity the class will have each six (6) week period will depend on the time of day the class meets each year in relation to other classes taught that period and gym space available. These are some suggested activities for the course.

1. Fitness Testing three times a year.
2. Fitness Center (weight training-circuit training)
3. Volleyball
4. Swimming / Water Walking/Aquarobics
   (ideal for at least two, six (6) week sessions or more)
5. Badminton
6. Aerobics (low impact)
7. Fitness Walking or Power Walking
8. Basketball
9. Fitness Trail
10. Softball
11. Soccer
12. Tennis

Program Results

The Physical Management Program created an awareness in the district of how the physical education teacher can play an important role in the treatment of adolescent obesity.

There has been a steady increase in the number enrolled in this class since its inception when it was first offered as a pilot project. There has been success in making the class attractive to the student who feels uncomfortable in regular class, and to those who would like some help in working on lifestyle changes.

One of the sections offered had 33 students and was strictly voluntary in nature. Eighteen of these students were repeating the course, some for the 3rd or 4th time. For many of these students, this class was the beginning of long term involvement with exercise. Last year a class of 22 students lost 127 lbs. by the end of the year. There was a significant improvement in each student's general fitness as measured by yearly assessments, especially in the area of cardiovascular fitness. However, it is important to note that unless the student maintains a reasonably active lifestyle once the program has ended, the beneficial effects of the program will be short lived.

Future program goals include recruiting a section for males and expanding the program into additional high schools.

ESTIMATING DAILY ENERGY NEEDS

The method outlined here provides an easy and practical approach to estimating daily calorie (energy) needs. While it is a rough estimate, it will serve to aid students in learning the concepts of calorie expenditure (Kcal–usually pronounced calories).

FIRST Estimate Basal Metabolic Energy Needs (BMR = Basal Metabolic Rate)

STEPS

1. Change pounds to kilograms:

   $$\frac{\text{weight in pounds}}{2.2} = \text{kg}$$

2. Multiply kg weight times BMR factor:
   1.0 kcal/kg/hr. for males
   .9 kcal/kg/hr for females

3. Multiply the kcalories used in one hour by the hours in a day

EXAMPLES

1. A 150 pound woman $\frac{150}{2.2} = 68$ kg.

   $150 \div 2.2 = 68$

2. $68 \times .9 = 61$ kcal per hour

3. $61 \times 24 = 1464$ kcal per day for BMR

SECOND Estimate Physical Activity Energy Needs

4. Determine the percentage of the BMR depending on a person's lifestyle in terms of muscular activity
   a. Sedentary person (mostly sitting) add 20% of BMR
   b. Light activity add 30% of BMR
   c. Moderate activity add 40% of BMR
   d. Heavy work add 50% of BMR

5. Add **BMR** kcal and activity

4. Our 150 pound woman is a sedentary typist:

   1464 kcal per day x 20% = 293 kcal per day for physical activity

5. $1464 + 293 = 1757$

THIRD Estimate energy need for specific dynamic effect of food (SDE)–the energy spent on digestion and metabolism of food

6. Find 10% of total kcalories per day in step 5

6. $1757 \times 10\% = 176$ kcal

FOURTH

Determine full day's estimate energy needs.

7. Add kcalories for BMR, physical activity and SDE

7. BMR = 1464
   Activity = 293
   SDE = 176
   24 hour total...1933 kcal

S A M P L E

Week of _____   **Name**_____

EXERCISE LOG SHEET
Record minutes or repetitions

AEROBICS	MON.	TUES.	WED.	THUR.	FRI.
STAIR MACHINE					
EXERCISE BIKE					
JUMP ROPE					
ROWING					
SWIMMING					
BIKE					
AEROBIC DANCE					
WALK/JOG					
OTHER					
ARMS	**MON.**	**TUES.**	**WED.**	**THUR.**	**FRI.**
MACHINES					
PUSH-UPS					
PULL-UP BAR					
REVERSE DIPS					
SURGICAL TUBING					
HAND WEIGHTS					
OTHER					
ABDOMINALS	**MON.**	**TUES.**	**WED.**	**THUR.**	**FRI.**
SIT-UPS					
CRUNCHES					
R & L OBLIQUES (Side Bends)					
KNEE LIFTS (Hip Flexor Machine)					
ALTERNATE KNEES					
OTHER					
LEGS	**MON.**	**TUES.**	**WED.**	**THUR.**	**FRI.**
MACHINES					
BANDS					
OTHER					

S A M P L E

Week of _____ **Name** _____

EXERCISE LOG SHEET
Record minutes or repetitions

AEROBICS	MON.	TUES.	WED.	THUR.	FRI.

ARMS	MON.	TUES.	WED.	THUR.	FRI.

ABDOMINALS	MON.	TUES.	WED.	THUR.	FRI.

LEGS	MON.	TUES.	WED.	THUR.	FRI.

SAMPLE

Personal Exercise Log

day	exercise mode	warm-up duration	exercise duration	cool-down duration	exercise HR	comments
Sun						
Mon						
Tue						
Wed						
Thu						
Fri						
Sat						

goals for next week:

SAMPLE

Assessment Chart
PHYSICAL MANAGEMENT

Name _____ **Class** _____

Date	Weight	Body Fat%	Mile Run	Sit & Reach	Push-ups	Sit-ups	Step Test

SAMPLE

SAMPLE

MUSCULAR FITNESS PROGRAM PLANNING FORM

Name ——————— Date ——— Class ———

Body Part	Exercise	Resistance	Repetitions	Sets

Comments:

SAMPLE

CARDIOVASCULAR FITNESS RECORD
(IS YOUR HEART GETTING STRONGER?)

Target Zone (65%-80%)

130 Beats/min.-**165** Beats/min.

21/10 sec.-**27**/10 sec.

Use the **F.I.T.** formula in order to improve the following.

FREQUENCY (How often)

INTENSITY (How hard)

TIME (How long)

DATE	RESTING PULSE RATE	DATE	RECOVERY RATE (5 Min.)

DATE	BLOOD PRESSURE	DATE	BEST MILE TIME

SAMPLE

PHYSICAL MANAGEMENT

Name _____ Class _____

Date/ WT.	Date/ WT.	Date/ WT.	Date/ WT.	Date/ WT.	Date/ WT.	Date/ WT.	Date/ WT.	Date/ WT.	Date/ WT.

Weight Graph

Weight

+20
+18
+16
+14
+12
+10
+8
+6
+4
+2
Start Weight
-2
-4
-6
-8
-10
-12
-14
-16
-18
-20

Date

SAMPLE

LIFESTYLE GOALS

Week #

New Goal

#		1	2	3	4	5	6	7	8	9	10	11	12	13	14	15	16	17	18	19	20	21
1.																						
2.																						
3.																						
4.																						
5.																						
6.																						
7.																						
8.																						
9.																						
10.																						
11.																						
12.																						
13.																						
14.																						
15.																						
16.																						
17.																						
18.																						
19.																						
20.																						

About the Editor and the Sporting Goods Manufacturers Association

Fitness consultant Lynn Allen is the president of Heartland Fitness in Cedar Falls, Iowa. A founding member of the Iowa Youth Fitness Task Force, in 1994 she was appointed to the Iowa Governor's Council on Physical Fitness and Sports. Lynn works as a clinician and instructor on behalf of the President's Council on Physical Fitness and Sports and as an advisor to the Fitness Products Council of the Sporting Goods Manufacturers Association.

Lynn developed the Universal Fitness Institute (a four-day fitness certification course) for Universal Gym Equipment and has conducted the course throughout the United States, Europe, Australia, and the Pacific Rim. In addition, she has conducted fitness clinics for the U.S. military, the Australian military, and the Singapore Army. In 1993 Lynn designed an exercise room in the White House for President and Mrs. Clinton and developed personal exercise programs for each of them.

Lynn earned her bachelor's degree in recreational education with emphasis in corporate fitness from the University of Iowa in 1981. She lives in Cedar Falls with her husband, Terry, and their daughter, Angela.

The Sporting Goods Manufacturers Association (SGMA) comprises 14 nonprofit associations, councils, and committees that share a common goal of preserving and advancing recreational sports in the United States. Founded in 1906, the SGMA works to increase amateur sports participation.

SGMA owns THE SUPER SHOW®, the world's largest trade show of sporting goods equipment, apparel, and accessories. Proceeds from THE SUPER SHOW support a host of national and local nonprofit sports organizations and programs. These funds are also used to sponsor many surveys and educational initiatives to benefit recreational sports.